TREATING
OBSESSIVE-COMPULSIVE
DISORDER

Pergamon Titles of Related Interest

Agras/EATING DISORDERS: Management of Obesity, Bulimia and Anorexia Nervosa

Becker/Heimberg/Bellack/SOCIAL SKILLS TRAINING TREATMENT FOR DEPRESSION

Gotlib/Colby/ TREATMENT OF DEPRESSION: An Interpersonal Systems Approach

Meichenbaum/STRESS INOCULATION TRAINING

Weiss/Katzman/Wolchik/ TREATING BULIMIA: A Psychoeducational Approach

Related Journals*

BEHAVIOUR RESEARCH AND THERAPY

BEHAVIORAL ASSESSMENT

CLINICAL PSYCHOLOGY REVIEW

JOURNAL OF BEHAVIOR THERAPY AND EXPERIMENTAL PSYCHIATRY

*Free sample copies available upon request

PSYCHOLOGY PRACTITIONER GUIDEBOOKS

EDITORS
Arnold P. Goldstein, Syracuse University
Leonard Krasner, Stanford University & SUNY at Stony Brook
Sol L. Garfield, Washington University in St. Louis

TREATING OBSESSIVE-COMPULSIVE DISORDER

SAMUEL M. TURNER
DEBORAH C. BEIDEL
University of Pittsburgh School of Medicine

PERGAMON PRESS
New York · Oxford · Beijing · Frankfurt
São Paulo · Sydney · Tokyo · Toronto

U.S.A.	Pergamon Press, Inc., Maxwell House, Fairview Park, Elmsford, New York 10523, U.S.A.
U.K.	Pergamon Press plc, Headington Hill Hall, Oxford OX3 0BW, England
PEOPLE'S REPUBLIC OF CHINA	Pergamon Press, Room 4037, Qianmen Hotel, Beijing, People's Republic of China
FEDERAL REPUBLIC OF GERMANY	Pergamon Press GmbH, Hammerweg 6, D-6242 Kronberg, Federal Republic of Germany
BRAZIL	Pergamon Editora Ltda, Rua Eça de Queiros, 346, CEP 04011, Paraiso, São Paulo, Brazil
AUSTRALIA	Pergamon Press Australia Pty Ltd., P.O. Box 544, Potts Point, N.S.W. 2011, Australia
JAPAN	Pergamon Press, 5th Floor, Matsuoka Central Building, 1-7-1 Nishishinjuku, Shinjuku-ku, Tokyo 160, Japan
CANADA	Pergamon Press Canada Ltd., Suite No. 271, 253 College Street, Toronto, Ontario, Canada M5T 1R5

First edition 1988

Library of Congress Cataloging in Publication Data
Turner, Samuel M., 1944–
Treating obsessive-compulsive disorder.
(Psychology practitioner guidebooks)
Bibliography: p.
Includes index.
1. Obsessive-compulsive neurosis—Treatment.
I. Beidel, Deborah C. II. Title. III. Series.
[DNLM: 1. Obsessive-Compulsive Disorder—therapy.
WM 176 T952t]
RC533.T87   1988   616.85′22706   87–29257

British Library Cataloguing in Publication Data
Turner, Samuel M.
Treating obsessive-compulsive disorder.
(Psychology practitioner guidebooks).
1. Obsessive-compulsive neurosis
2. Behavior therapy
I. Title II. Beidel, Deborah C.
III. Series
616.85′227   RC533

ISBN 0–08–034232–9 (Hardcover)
ISBN 0–08–034231–0 (Flexicover)

Printed in Great Britain by A. Wheaton & Co. Ltd., Exeter

Contents

Preface

Obsessive–compulsive disorder (OCD) was once considered a relatively rare condition and highly refractory to treatment. In recent years, significant progress has been made in the treatment of this extremely debilitating disorder. Behavioral treatments consisting primarily of various methods of exposure and response prevention are reported to be approximately 70% effective in treating this condition. Moreover, a number of follow-up studies of patients treated with behavioral methods have shown that, in many cases, the effectiveness of these interventions persists over a number of years (e.g., Kirk, 1983). Psychopharmacological treatment with antidepressant drugs, particularly those with strong serotonergic action, also has shown promising results. In some cases it appears that a combination of the two modalities might constitute the optimal treatment regimen. Some investigators (Foa, Steketee, & Ozarow, 1985) have concluded that behavioral procedures embodying exposure principles are now the treatments of choice for obsessional states. Although we concur with their assessment, much remains to be done in refining these strategies and determining which patients are most likely to respond to these interventions.

Patients suffering from obsessions and compulsions were once thought to be rather rare. However, the most recent epidemiological data suggest that the prevalence of the disorder in the general population is about 2%. This means that there are approximately 490,000 obsessional patients in the United States, and it also means that there are at least as many obsessional patients as there are schizophrenics. We believe that, once the availability of treatments for obsessive–compulsive disorder is made known to the general public, there will be a steady increase in the number of obsessional patients seeking treatment, much as was the case when treatments for agoraphobia became popular.

Although we know that there are effective treatments for this condition, at the present there are only a few major treatment centers for the disorder in the United States. Furthermore, the treatment interventions are highly specialized and quite time consuming, and few therapists in private practice or in mental health clinics have sufficient expertise or time to carry out a treatment program for obsessional patients. One goal we have for this book is to acquaint clinicians with the currently effective treatments for obsessive–compulsive disorder so that they will at least have a conceptual understanding of how the treatments are carried out. For those with the appropriate background, the volume might actually help them construct treatment plans for their patients. A second goal is to provide information for graduate students and other trainees that will aid their understanding of obsessional patients, the treatments that have proven effective, and their preparation to engage in the treatment of such patients.

This volume is one of a series of works that are primarily designed to address the treatment of a variety of disorders. In fact, many of the titles, including this one, can be considered treatment manuals. Although treatment manuals can no doubt serve a valuable training function, and might be particularly useful in treatment-outcome studies, there is a major limitation that should be illuminated. No matter how detailed and complete a manual might be, the actual implementation of an intervention with a particular patient requires considerable clinical expertise and judgment on the part of the therapist. Moreover, alteration of the set plan needs to be made in some cases. Therefore, the possession of a treatment manual does not guarantee that one has a step-by-step treatment plan that will lead to a successful outcome. Nothing can take the place of an adequately trained clinician who can adapt a particular strategy to a specific patient.

In perusing this book, the reader will note that we have limited our discussion of treatments for obsessional states to behavioral and pharmacological interventions. Our reason for doing so is quite simple. The available literature on the treatment of this disorder clearly indicates that these interventions are effective. We know of no empirical basis for the use of other types of interventions other than perhaps psychosurgery, a radical form of treatment we believe to be unnecessary. We do provide a brief discussion of psychosurgery in chapter 6.

We have attempted to describe the syndrome (chapter 1), the diagnostic issues (chapter 2), the assessment strategies and patient management (chapter 3), the behavioral treatments (chapter 4), the specifics for implementing behavioral treatments (chapter 5), the biological treatments (chapter 6), and the maintenance issues (chapter 7). Several of these chapters are written in a somewhat unusual fashion. Chapter 1 contains a firsthand account of the development and progression of an obsessional state by a patient treated in our clinic. This account vividly describes the pervasiveness of the disorder, the suffering and the sense of hopelessness experienced by the patient, and the impact of the disorder on her family. This same patient provides (in chapter 4) an account of her experience going through treatment in our clinic. This information should prove to be enlightening for those who have had little experience with obsessionals. The patient accepted our invitation to write these sections because she wanted others to know what her experience had been like, and she hoped that her story might inspire others in need of treatment. The decision to do this required a great amount of courage, and we salute her for her effort and her family for their encouragement and support.

It is our hope that the information contained in this volume might play some small role in educating the mental health community about the nature of obsessional states. Moreover, if this work can aid in the elimination of the still widely held belief that obsessional states are untreatable, our efforts will have been well worthwhile.

Samuel M. Turner

Deborah C. Beidel

Pittsburgh, Pennsylvania

Chapter 1
Clinical Syndrome

Obsessive–compulsive disorder is a complex clinical syndrome that usually causes considerable overall distress. The disorder is characterized by the presence of obsessive ideation, typically accompanied by overt behavioral acts carried out in ritualistic fashion. Jaspers (1963) provided an apt description of the disorder when he characterized the condition as an incessant preoccupation with impulses and anxiety that the individual experiences as groundless, senseless, and impossible.

CLINICAL DESCRIPTION

Obsessions are thoughts, images, ideas, and impulses that persistently invade the consciousness. In some cases these cognitive phenomena are present on a continual basis; in other instances they are episodic, or cued by various types of stimuli including environmental, psychological and physical events. Once they are present, the individual feels unable to control or eliminate them. When these cognitive events occur, the individual is unable to explain them and often views them as repugnant, senseless, frightening, and not reflective of his or her true feelings. Although there is sometimes an element of rationality to the fears (e.g., possible contamination), the extent of the fear is usually recognized as irrational by everyone concerned including the patient. Some individuals report very specific types of thoughts such as "I love Satan," "I want to kill my wife," or "I ran over someone with my car," whereas others experience a vague sense of dread that something terrible is about to happen. Alternatively, there might be apprehension that some specific event will occur, such as the burning of a house, the contracting of a terminal illness, or the causing of another's death by contamination or negligence. Akhtar, Wig, Verna, Pershod, and Verna (1975) found that dirt and contamination

1

were the most common content of obsessions, followed in descending order by aggression and violence, religion, and sex.

Obsessional visual images can include seeing oneself engage in a despicable act or visualizing something terrible happening to a loved one. Thus, a recent patient treated in our clinic was plagued with the image of plunging a knife into his father's chest. Similarly, another patient continually visualized placing a blanket over the face of her newborn child and suffocating her. It is important to note here that the possible content of obsessional material is endless. Thus, the critical factor is not the substance but the intrusive nature of the phenomena, the recognition that it is senseless, and its ability to create distress for the individual. It is sometimes difficult to apply these criteria, and we will discuss some of the problems in our exploration of differential diagnosis in chapter 2.

Compulsions are overt or covert acts that, for the most part, appear to be associated with the presence of obsessions. These acts are typically carried out in ritualized or stereotyped fashion and are generally referred to as compulsive rituals. Although active resistance on the part of the individual was once considered essential to the diagnosis of OCD, it is now recognized that resistance is not always discernible. The absence of resistance can be found mainly in very chronic cases and no doubt results in part from many years of fruitless effort at controlling the behavior.

Common rituals include excessive handwashing and bathing, cleaning, checking and rechecking of various household appliances, door and window locks, work-related material and items viewed as safety hazards. Washing and cleaning rituals are usually related to some type of contamination fear, whereas checking typically reflects doubt about personal performance or fear of being held responsible for some dreaded catastrophic event.

Checking and washing behavior is frequently severe and can occupy all of the waking hours. In extreme cases, the individual even remains awake for as much of the night as possible to continue ritualistic behaviors. We have also seen cases in which the patient felt the night hours were the only time that cleaning could be accomplished in a satisfactory manner. In one extremely severe case, a female patient remained awake as much of the night as possible to engage in cleaning designed to eliminate asbestos. What sleep she got was frequently during the day. Another patient currently in treatment in our clinic is a man who cannot complete his work requirements because he repeatedly checks and rechecks his work to ensure that it is perfect. In some instances, checking is associated with "magical numbers" such that a given item must be checked in some manner for a specific number of times; for example, checking the door lock while pulling on the knob and counting to three. These rituals frequently become intricate and time consuming, such as when numerous household items have to be checked or when one series of checking is insufficient. An example of this is needing to count to three for a series of nine times. A recent case in our clinic involved a man who felt the necessity to check and recheck the route he drove his car due to fear that he had somehow run over a child. This resulted in the necessity to cover the same route over and over again. Even upon arriving home, he would phone hospitals and police stations to assuage his fear of having hurt someone. The disorder became so severe that relatives were enlisted to help in the checking behavior.

Rituals can also be purely cognitive. A cognitive ritual is defined as a mental act carried out in a specific fashion and consisting of a number of discrete steps. Examples include reciting a prayer, visualizing a particular image, and reciting a series of statements or a sequence of numbers. These are different from obsessions in that they have a particular end point (Sturgis & Meyer, 1981). Like the content of obsessions, the behaviors comprising a ritual can be any act the person is capable of performing. The important point is that they are purposeful. For example, to the patient they might serve to prevent contamination, to ensure perfection, or to ward off catastrophic events.

Most rituals are viewed as a form of active or passive avoidance. In the case of the compulsive washer or cleaner, the ritual is a form of passive avoidance, and the act can be seen as serving a restorative function (i.e., the cleaning removes the contaminant). On the other hand, checking rituals are a form of active avoidance in that the behavior serves to prevent the occurrence of some catastrophic event. Patients can be afflicted with one or more patterns of rituals.

Most experts consider rituals to be associated with particular obsessions. The presence of the obsession leads to an uncontrollable urge to engage in certain behaviors. From the behavioral standpoint, rituals have been viewed as serving an anxiety-reduction function. Whether or not the performance of a ritual is associated with the reduction of anxiety has been a point of contention. For example, Walker and Beech (1969), among others, have shown that there is sometimes an increase in anxiety and distress following the occurrence of ritualistic behavior. On the other hand, Rachman and his colleagues (e.g., Rachman, 1985) have clearly demonstrated that, for the majority of washers and checkers, rituals result in a reduction of anxiety. One reason why, for some individuals, rituals serve to increase anxiety is that the anxiety could be due to the patient's response to failure in controlling the rituals. Thus, immediately after performing the ritual, the individual engages in negative self-appraisal.

Table 1.1. Mean Scores of Anxiety Disorders Groups on Several Self-Report Instruments

Measure	Panic Disorder with Agoraphobia (n = 12)	Panic Disorder without Agoraphobia (n = 9)	Agoraphobia without Panic (n = 6)	GAD (n =9)	OCD (n = 9)	Social Phobia (n = 12)	Simple Phobia (n = 32)
State–Trait Anxiety Inventory							
A-state	51.6	48.3	50.0	56.6	62.9	45.0	34.6
A-trait	50.0	48.8	55.5	63.2	63.1	43.2	35.6
Maudsley Obsessive–Compulsive Inventory	7.3	7.5	10.2	9.1	16.8	6.3	4.5
Fear Survey Schedule	134.4	122.7	168.7	145.6	154.6	72.7	64.7
Social Avoidance and Distress Scale	18.8	21.0	16.3	17.8	13.7	13.4	5.6
Fear of Negative Evaluation Scale	20.3	17.5	17.8	20.1	19.3	20.9	9.7
Beck Depression Inventory	15.6	17.7	19.7	22.7	25.0	8.8	9.0

Note. Adapted from: "DSM-III Classification of the Anxiety Disorders: A Psychometric Study", by S. M. Turner, B. S. McCann, D. C. Beidel, and J. E. Mezzich, 1986, Journal of Abnormal Psychology, 95, p. 169.

Normally, rituals are associated with specific obsessional ideation. However, they sometimes become disassociated from the obsession and appear to be autonomous. We have seen a small number of such cases and agree with Walton and Mather (1963) that this is most likely to occur in instances where the disorder takes a particularly chronic course or the patient has an extremely pervasive disorder and such ambivalence that she or he simply cannot decide how the obsessions and compulsions are related.

Rachman (1974) described what appears to be a form of obsessional disorder he termed *primary obsessional slowness*. The syndrome is characterized by extreme slowness in completing various acts such as dressing in the morning or completing a certain work assignment. These behaviors are apparently completed without association to a specific ritual and are not followed by subsequent anxiety reduction. R. S. Stern and Cobb (1978) described the condition as one characterized by completeness and meticulousness of thought. It is unclear if this is some type of variant of OCD or if this represents a segment of the continuum between OCD and compulsive personality disorder. In our own experience, most patients showing this pattern also have other obsessions and compulsions, and we believe it is rare for this pattern to occur alone.

Individuals suffering from obsessions and compulsions usually report the existence of chronic maladaptive anxiety and various degrees of depression. Anxiety might be manifested by general nervousness, apprehension, irritability, restlessness, and, frequently, numerous somatic complaints and some form of self-doubt that often appears as ambivalence or indecisiveness. Panic attacks occur at high frequency in obsessional patients and can be triggered by specific stimuli or be of the spontaneous variety. In almost all instances, there is a pervasive pattern of worrying, and patients frequently state that, if they do not have anything to worry about, they create something, adding to a picture of mass apprehensiveness. Among anxiety-disorders patients, the obsessional patients appear to have the greatest amount of anxiety and the most pervasive pattern of fear (S. M. Turner, McCann, Beidel, & Mezzich, 1986; see Table 1.1).

CLINICAL COURSE

With the pervasive clinical picture we have described here, it should not be surprising that family, interpersonal, social, and occupational functioning are often disturbed. We do not wish to convey the impression that all obsessionals present with all of these symptoms in their severest form. But they are usually present in some degree and tend to worsen over the course of the disorder.

The most common course of OCD is that of a chronic, unremitting disturbance. Yet there are a minority of cases characterized by an episodic course. Some clarification of the concept of episodicity, however, is needed. Once the full-blown syndrome of OCD has been triggered, in our experience, it is unlikely that the individuals will ever be totally symptom free. Thus, the period between episodes is really characterized by a very low level of symptom intensity that might not cause serious distress nor interfere in any way with interpersonal relationships or occupational functioning. This is much like the histories many patients report prior to the initial onset of OCD. Strictly speaking, then, this is not a true episodic course but merely the episodic occurrence of peak intensity of the various symptoms.

ONSET

OCD is considered an early-adult-onset disorder, with the peak period occurring between the ages of 18 and 25. For example, Ingram (1961) and Pollitt (1957) reported the mean age of onset to be in the early 20s. Black (1974) reported that over 50% of his sample of OCD patients developed the disorder by age 25; 84%, by age 35. Rachman and Hodgson (1980) noted that the disorder seemed to have a "window of vulnerability" associated with early adulthood. It should be noted, however, that OCD is known to occur in children (Rapoport, 1986). Moreover, our experience suggests that elements of the disorder are present long before the full-blown syndrome appears. Usually, the symptoms occur on a sporadic basis, are of such low intensity as not to be problematic or cause the individual distress, or appear so insignificant that the individual does not pay them much attention. Finally, the early "prodromal" sign might consist mainly of behavior comprising the obsessive–compulsive personality syndrome. The earliest onset of a frank compulsive disorder that we have witnessed occurred in the 4-year-old son of an OCD patient undergoing treatment in our clinic. Although onset in later life is possible, in our experience this usually occurs in individuals who have had characteristics of the disorder for many years but are now unable to contain them, or it worsens as the result of some type of stress. A number of different types of stressors have been associated with the onset of OCD, and these include medical illness, childbirth, and various forms of interpersonal and occupational stress. As we will point out in our discussion of maintenance of treatment in chapter 6, following the onset, the disorder can wax and wane with the existence or severity of the stressors.

ADDITIONAL CLINICAL PHENOMENA

Obsessional patients typically report some degree of dysphoria. This ranges in intensity from distress over lack of ability to control various behaviors to severe depression and suicidal ideation or attempts. Usually these patients are somewhere between the extremes, reporting sleep difficulty, anergia, and loss of ability to concentrate. In a study conducted in our clinic, obsessional patients were found to experience a more severe degree of distress than any other anxiety-disorders patient, as measured by self-report inventories (see Table 1.1).

Additionally, obsessional patients often present with a myriad of interpersonal, marital, and family problems, as well as difficulties centered around academic or occupational activities. In fact, it is sometimes the demands from family members or employers that force obsessional patients to seek treatment. For example, one patient with a long history of many obsessions and compulsions only sought treatment when his employer informed him that, in order to keep his job, he would have to enter treatment. Similarly, we recently assessed an obsessive patient who had traveled over 1,000 miles to our clinic but who had not decided that he really needed treatment. His decision to seek an opinion on his condition came at the insistence of his wife, and his decision to travel so far for a consultation was partly due to his desire to ensure that no one he knew would find out about it.

In some cases, it is difficult to determine whether these difficulties are a result of the obsessional disorder or contributors to the development of the disorder. In the majority of cases, both alternatives are usually true. Although the onset of obsessive-compulsive disorder frequently follows some type of stress (e.g., family or marital discord, employment demands, childbirth, or other physical stress such as disease), in our experience, obsessional characteristics often contribute to the development of many of these problems as well. Trying to disentangle the causality before the obsessions and compulsions are under control is probably a useless exercise. We have found that intervention in other areas is not likely to be successful before the primary disorder is treated. We believe the cases of acute onset of obsessional disorder without some precursory behavior are relatively rare. That is to say, various characteristics of the disorder appear to be present prior to the full-blown syndrome. Usually these characteristics were dismissed as simple quirks by the patient and others because they simply did not interfere in a significant way or did not cause personal distress. In some instances the behaviors were noted to be abnormal but still did not significantly interfere with normal functioning. It is our experience that elements of the syndrome can be detected in the early childhood years or at various stages of development during the adolescent years. Careful and specific questioning of the patient and significant others is often required to detect these early behaviors.

To summarize, the clinical picture of the obsessive–compulsive patient is often one of significant overall distress. The patient suffers from considerable general anxiety, is depressed, and might be afflicted by any number or combination of obsessions and rituals. In addition, the patient's personal life frequently is in total disarray. To complicate matters further, the patient's ambivalence and hostility often make it difficult for him or her to decide to enter treatment and for the therapist to cope with the patient.

Next, we go to some length to provide a first-person account of the experience with OCD in a female patient treated in our clinic. The patient who is married, complained of a number of cleaning and washing rituals associated with obsessional ideation about contamination by germs. Specifically, the patient was afraid of being contaminated by animal hair. Her fear was so extreme that people who owned animals were not allowed into her home, nor were her children allowed to come into contact with animals. She took numerous precautions to ensure cleanliness, such as having her children disrobe in the garage so their clothing could be washed. There were a number of "safe zones" in her house that only she could enter.

At the time of her admission to our clinic, the behaviors had been present for about 7 or 8 years and had apparently existed prior to this, but at a lower level. She is a meticulous individual who always has been a perfectionist, as are her father and her sister. She had been seeing a therapist for 1 year prior to her contact with our clinic, with some improvement. In addition, there were significant marital distress and mild depressive symptoms, including suicidal ideation. We asked her to describe in her own words the development of the disorder. We believe this account illustrates most vividly what we have noted and provides considerable insight into how obsessional patients see their situation and how they view others. In subsequent chapters she will describe her feelings as she progresses through treatment (chapter 4) and her reflections on her life 1 year after treatment (chapter 7).

FIRST-PERSON DESCRIPTION
BY MRS. C.

It is difficult to say exactly when the obsessions and compulsions began. They happened gradually over a period of many years, but there were several events that seemed significant. In the fall of 1971, I can remember buying groceries at a large supermarket in Texas. I saw some roaches crawling over the meat counter. This disturbed me very much, as I had lived in the North all my life and had no idea roaches were so numerous in the South. When I got home, I wondered how many containers might have been in contact with the roaches. I decided to wash off all the groceries before putting them in the kitchen cabinets, and I finally felt they were clean enough. I continued doing this every time I brought food home for the next 14 years.

Another event occurred in the spring of 1974. I had borrowed some linen napkins from a friend, and they were covered with animal hairs. This disgusted me, and I did not want to use them for my dinner guests. In addition, we were living in an apartment, and, during humid weather, I began to notice the smell from my friend's pets in the apartment hallway and even by the door inside my own apartment. One day her half-grown German Shepherd followed her into my place. I can remember thinking to myself that I really did not want that animal in my kitchen. I felt relieved when she and the dog left. There were dog hairs on the floor, and, although I did not vacuum or scrub the floors, I was uncomfortable around animals after this incident occurred. I do not remember any anxiety around animals prior to these incidents. In fact, I had grown up enjoying animals, having had a cat as a pet and often visiting my grandparents' farm.

Later in 1974, a third event occurred when we moved to another apartment. I had always been concerned about cleaning new apartments, but looking back now, I see a change in myself at this point. The cleaning had become more ritualized. I had to use a disinfectant when I was cleaning the kitchen cabinets, and I scrubbed every square inch of the cabinets, both inside and out. I can remember thinking to myself that I was really getting good at this. I can also see now that the cleaning was relieving my anxiety. There were several stressors in my life at that time, and, as I completed the cabinets, I felt better. I now recognize that the cleaning compulsion was tension relieving, although I did not associate the two events at all at the time.

During the winter I became concerned about anything falling on the floor. I felt that, once something fell on the floor, it was dirty. I began washing things before replacing them on the kitchen counter, the end tables in the living room, or the dresser in the bedroom.

There are several behaviors I remember as a child between the ages of 6 and 8 that I now see as related to my problem. While riding in the family car and looking out the window, I would imagine the car jumping over the telephone poles along the road, one after another. It started out innocently enough, but, when I tried to stop imagining it, I could not. It became very annoying to me. I would want to just look out the window, but I kept seeing and feeling the car jumping over the poles. I would even close my eyes, but the same image remained.

At this age I also remember engaging in repetitive finger and jaw movements. I would move each finger in a certain pattern. However, when I eventually wanted to stop the finger movements, I could not. I had to complete the certain pattern before I could stop. Even then, sometimes I had to keep doing it over and over again. The jaw movements were similar. I would grind my teeth on one side and then the other in a similar pattern. This was also something I could not stop, no matter how hard I tried. Many years later, when I learned what obsessions and compulsions were, I realized this was what I had been doing.

I believe a contributing factor to my later obsession with cleanliness was the emphasis in nursing school on isolation techniques in infectious disease, sterile procedures in the operating room, and the concept of clean or sterile versus contaminated. If a contaminated object touched a clean object, the clean object was then contaminated also. I learned to use these procedures in the nursery, where we washed every infant's bassinet and supplies with disinfectant daily; in the delivery room, where we washed containers and shelves with disinfectant; and in the operating room, where we gowned, masked, and scrubbed before entering. Carrying out these aseptic procedures was a large part of my life during my 3 years of nursing school and 2 years of employment as a registered nurse. I was very involved in trying to do each procedure just right and later became too involved when I allowed it to enter my personal and professional lives.

From the time I first began washing groceries in the winter of 1971 until I first explained my problem to a psychologist in 1984, the time occupied by my thoughts and behavior associated with cleanliness escalated from a few minutes a day to about 18 hours a day. With the birth of my first child in 1976, I was very careful to make sure everything that went into his mouth or was next to his skin was clean. I also told everyone to wash before holding him. Of course, I was also very careful about washing not only bottles in hot, soapy water, but also cans of formula and baby-food jars before opening them. Then, when he started playing with toys and putting them in his mouth, I washed every toy he came in contact with. When a toy fell on the floor, I washed it again. My anxiety over watching my child put something that had been on the floor into his mouth was so intense that I had to keep washing everything. I also knew babies needed the experience of crawling on the floor and exploring, so I structured my life around making sure everything in the baby's environment was clean.

The first time I brought my son home from a checkup with the pediatrician I went to lay him in his crib. Right away I thought of all the other children who had been in the office and on the examining table where he had been, and I could not lay him in his bed on his clean sheet. I gave him a bath and dressed him in clean clothes. This ritual continued for all my children whenever they left the house and returned home. It also included washing their hair every night before they went to bed.

My anxiety spread further when I began taking my baby for visits to friends and family. To begin with, at nursing school I had learned about the spread of pinworms from pet dogs to babies and children in the family. When I took my baby to visit a friend who had a pet dog, everything I had learned came back to me. I saw her dog sniff at me and my baby, lick her children, and jump on them. I noticed dog hairs around the house, and I could smell the dog. I saw areas outside where the dog had defecated in the grass. All of this was on my mind when I was leaving and driving home with my baby. I began to feel we were both contaminated with this dog. In my car at some point, I decided to bathe my son and put clean clothes on him as soon as we were home. I washed the diaper bag and everything that was in it, and I changed my own clothes. By then I felt like he was clean enough and, as I look back now, my anxiety was relieved. The cleaning continued every time we visited people who had a pet in their house, and over a period of time, generalized to include washing out the inside of the car and the baby's car seat. When I had more children, I had three to bathe, as well as three coats and three sets of clothes to wash.

My fears continued to spread so that I could no longer have friends with pets come into my home without carrying out elaborate cleaning rituals afterward. At first, after friends with pets would leave, I would wash only the toys and the playpen. Later my ritual grew to scrubbing and vacuuming the floors where they had walked, washing the chairs where they had sat, washing the walls and woodwork they had touched, and washing all the toys my children accumulated. I did not know anymore which toys their children had touched, so I washed them all. I felt like I had to eliminate any animal hair or dirt that might have been transferred from their pets onto them and into my house.

There was a period of time when I only cleaned when I knew for certain they had a pet. Then, in the last few years before my treatment, I could no longer do that. I realized that people who do not own pets are sometimes in contact with animals. I began to get very anxious whenever anyone was in my home. I also began to get anxious outside of my home when my children or I brushed against someone on the street or in a public place. I felt like I had to go home and wash.

One of my worst experiences occurred in February 1984, after we had moved into a new home. Our three children were ages 8, 5, and 5 months. We had packed and moved all of our household items, except furniture. Almost everything was stored in the attic or the basement prior to our move, so the boxes would not interfere with the contractor who was finishing the house. We had the furniture arranged and were getting settled in the house when I started removing boxes from the attic. One sunny afternoon, after I had spent the morning unpacking boxes from the attic, I was holding the baby, sitting on the couch and looking out of the window at the woods. Suddenly, I heard a noise that sounded like the branch of a tree on the roof. For an instant, I thought to myself that there could have been a mouse in the attic, and I could not get rid of this idea. When I opened the attic door and saw the droppings, I knew there had been a mouse.

From that moment on my anxiety level began climbing higher, until it was almost unbearable. I began to worry that the mouse had been in the rest of the house too. I was afraid it might be running over my children's beds, toys, and clothing; my kitchen cabinets; anywhere. Next, I thought about all those boxes in the attic that I had not unpacked yet. The mouse could have been in any of them, and, because I did not know which, I would have to wash everything before we could use it; all the toys and games, the children's books, out-of-season clothing for all five of us, clothing that my older children had outgrown and that I was saving for the baby, kitchen utensils, canning jars and supplies, and Christmas decorations. The list went on and on. There were so many boxes up there, and I was feeling overwhelmed. I could not imagine how I was going to clean anything, but I would have to before I could put these things away and feel relief from all this anxiety and feel like this house was home. Then, I began to think about the boxes I had already gotten out of the attic. I really didn't know if the mouse had been in those or not. Even if it hadn't been inside the boxes, it might have crawled on the outsides. My children had certainly touched the outsides of the boxes of toys, and, then, when they had touched the toys inside the boxes, the insides would be dirty too. Whatever else in the house they touched before washing their hands would also be dirty.

This was how my thought processes were working. I was not able to change it. I kept getting more and more anxious. I was feeling despair and could see no way out of this situation except to clean and wash everything. I was also under pressure from my family. My children wanted their toys, so I washed the toys and then I washed their hands. I made them promise never to go into the attic until I cleaned it. I pleaded with my husband to not go into the attic until it was clean. I never knew for certain if he would go in or not, and I worried about this for months afterward. Finally, I resolved this by never leaving the house myself when he was at home. I was so afraid he might go into the attic and track mouse hair onto the carpet.

When the compulsions were most severe, most of my time was spent in cleaning rituals or in thinking about the rituals. I continued the house-work in our new home and the care of our three children while always trying to find time to get back to the rituals. My life was limited in many ways. My social relationships were limited to friends who did not own pets. I was afraid every time the telephone rang that a friend who had a pet might be inviting me to her home or might want to visit me in my home. When holidays were approaching, I was afraid relatives or friends who owned pets would want to visit. I was also tense over trying to hide my concern about animals and dirt from all these people. I tried very hard to pretend everything was fine, when inside I felt like exploding. I went to bed at night thinking about what I needed to wash the next day. Then there were also the times I would keep myself awake at night so I could get up when everyone else was asleep and wash things.

After a period of time, I lost interest in visiting my own relatives who had pets. We had visited my grandparents frequently, and I had allowed my children to play with their cats. In the wintertime, the cats were still kept outside, and my children watched them from the house. However, one time we walked into my grandmother's kitchen, and the cat was there inside the house. The children ran to it immediately. I froze at the same time. I was oblivious to everything around me. I heard voices talking, but I had no idea what they were saying. They sounded so far away. All I could think of was how I was going to wash all of our clothes, winter coats, and the inside of the car after we went home. I planned the order of everything so I wouldn't miss one piece of clothing.

My problem grew worse. I could not buy furniture because I was afraid someone who had a pet had touched it in the store or the warehouse. I was also afraid the delivery men might have had a pet, and I would have to vacuum the floors they walked on and wash the walls they touched. I gave up piano lessons and could not keep in contact with my teacher because she had a dog. Our new house was by a wooded area, and I was always afraid an animal might be in the house. I kept a couple of traps set in the house and checked them often. I continued to wash the groceries, and then this spread to include everything we bought and brought into the house. This included books, paint cans, mail, newspapers, toys, tools, pictures, everything.

With all this tension over the years, I am sure I must have been irritable with my family. I always tried to have patience with my children.

Sometimes this was difficult for me, probably more difficult than had I not been involved in my compulsions. I am sure I was less tolerant of their normal childhood behavior. I always tried very hard to meet their needs for my attention before doing any cleaning, but I'm not sure I was successful during the last few months before my treatment.

I had tried to keep as much hidden from my family as I could. My son began to realize something was wrong when I made excuses for his friends with pets not being able to visit our home and when I washed his clothes and toys after he visited their home. It seemed to upset him even more once I was in treatment and he began to understand that what I was doing was not normal and was so much trouble for him.

There were several other ways my children were involved in my rituals. I always questioned the children when they were playing at one of their friend's homes as to whether the friend had a pet. I knew it was important for them to have friends to play with, so I was always looking for other children who did not have pets at home. They also had to wash their hands after reading library books or other books from school. They had to change their clothes right after school in case they had brushed against a friend who had a pet. I washed their valentines or anything else their friends gave them to bring home.

My husband was not free to invite his friends or relatives to our home. This did not seem to bother him until his sister and her family wanted to visit us. The first incident occurred 5 years before my treatment. They told us when they would be coming and that their dog would be with them. I kept going over in my mind what I would have to clean afterward and became more and more anxious. I was so upset as their arrival came closer that my husband finally called them and said I was ill. This turned out to be the truth. I really hated for him to do this, but I can still remember how relieved I was that they were not coming.

The next incident occurred just prior to the beginning of my treatment in October 1984. This time my husband's sister and her family were moving out of the state and wanted to see our new house before they left. They had two dogs in their home, and the thoughts of their coming to our house put me in a state of panic. I was so distraught that I could not sleep at night, and I wandered around the house in tears. I did not want to hurt my husband or his family by refusing to allow them to visit, but I just could not cope with their coming and my washing everything in the house including the floors, drapes, bedspreads, and walls after they left. My husband was thoroughly disgusted with me, but he talked to his sister and told her we had prior plans for the weekend she planned to come. I felt so much relief that they were no longer coming, but I was so very sorry that it had to be this way.

COMMENTARY

This vivid description illustrates the original development of the disorder, at least with respect to the intense experience, as well as the tendency for it to continue unchecked until nearly every aspect of functioning had been affected. In addition, it demonstrates that more than just the patient suffers. Family relationships are often compromised as they were in this case, and family activities suffer severe disruption. Mrs. C. made a concerted effort to assure that her children had some peer relationships, but it is clear that the social development of children could be affected as a result of the imposition of restrictions by the affected parent. Despite her efforts to ensure her family a normal existence, she was unable to do so. Although it was not described in the exposé presented here, the onset of this disorder came during considerable marital strife and dissatisfaction.

EPIDEMIOLOGY

Exact figures on the prevalence of OCD are somewhat elusive, owing to the lack of good epidemiologic data. In older studies, estimates of the prevalence have varied from 3% to 4.6% of all psychiatric patients (Beech & Vaughn, 1978) to 3% of all neurotic patients (Hare, Price, & Slater, 1971). The most recent data are provided by the results of the Epidemiologic Catchment Area Survey sponsored by the National Institute of Mental Health. The results of this study suggest that the prevalence of OCD in the population is 3% (Turns, 1985). This is considerably higher than the usual estimates of about 1%. We have reason to believe that the 3% figure is probably high because of problems with the instrument used in the study to make diagnoses. Nevertheless, we are not surprised that the disorder was found to be more prevalent than prior figures had indicated. We suspect the very low early prevalence figures would be partially due to the failure of some OCD patients to seek treatment, partly due to their secretive nature, and partly due to the belief that there was no treatment available to help them. If we estimate the true prevalence to be 2%, OCD would then be as common as schizophrenia. In any event, we can safely assume that the true prevalence rate lies somewhere between 1% and 3%.

PROGNOSIS

OCD has a reputation for being a most difficult disorder to treat. Moreover, patients with this disorder are considered to be difficult to manage, probably due to the presence of such characteristics as anger, hostility, and rigidity. We will deal with the problem of management of these patients with respect to assessment and treatment in chapter 3. In a sample of 90 patients, Kringlen (1965) found that only 20% had improved 13 to 20 years after treatment. However, Grimshaw (1965) reported a somewhat more optimistic picture by describing 40% of his sample as showing much improvement over 14 years of follow-up. With the introduction of structured behavioral treatments during the past 20 years, the prognosis has become considerably more optimistic. For example, Steketee, Foa, and Grayson (1982) reported the effectiveness of behavioral treatments embodying exposure to be about 70% to 80% effective. In a follow-up study of 36 patients over a period of 1 to 5 years, Kirk (1983) found that 81% of the patients treated had not required additional referral. These data are consistent with what we have seen in our clinic. Nevertheless, several points should be made in accepting these data as realistic figures for OCD patients with behavioral treatments. *First*, it is difficult to determine exactly what "significant improvement" means in the various studies, inasmuch as different procedures are often employed to make this determination. *Second*, we have noted that, even in our patients who are greatly improved, there remains a residual anxiety state. Therefore, we believe there is great likelihood that the disorder could recur under stressful conditions. We will discuss some of the issues related to improvement and the maintenance of improvement in our chapter on behavioral treatments.

SUMMARY

In summary, obsessive–compulsive disorder is a severe disturbance characterized by the presence of intrusive and disturbing cognitive phenomena in the form of thoughts, images, or impulses. In the majority of cases, these are accompanied by overt behavioral acts performed in ritualistic fashion, the most common of which are washing and checking. The disorder is accompanied by a number of other symptoms including anxiety and depression and usually significantly affects most areas of functioning. OCD patients are commonly angry and hostile and might show features of obsessive–compulsive personality. The disorder is considered an early-adult-onset disorder with a chronic course, most often of an unremitting nature but sometimes episodic. It is thought to affect somewhere between 1% and 3% of the population. Finally, although the prognosis has improved over the past 20 years, it still remains a notoriously difficult-to-treat disorder and one for which maintenance-of-treatment gains are difficult to attain. In addition to the residual anxiety state, obsessions and compulsions are rarely, if ever, totally eliminated. Thus, features of the disorder persist.

Chapter 2
Differential Diagnosis

Obsessive–compulsive disorder can be diagnosed when both obsessions and compulsions are present or when only obsessions exist. Given the clinical picture presented in chapter 1, one would expect this to be an easily recognized syndrome and one that should be diagnosed easily. Although some cases are indeed quickly recognized, there are those that present considerable difficulty, even for the experienced clinician. This is primarily due to overlap and similarity with other conditions.

A second problem has already been alluded to in chapter 1: the problem of OCD patients withholding information, failing to elucidate the entire symptom pattern, or minimizing symptom severity. Thus, OCD patients might seek treatment but not reveal the extent or even the presence of obsessions and compulsions because they view them as silly or forms of weakness, and they are embarrassed to discuss them. Instead, they might focus on symptoms of depression, or global feelings of anxiety or present with vague expressions of dissatisfaction with their lives.

To uncover the existence of obsessions and compulsions sometimes requires detailed questioning and recognition of the more subtle indicants of the disorder. Certainly, anyone suspected of having an anxiety disorder should be examined specifically for obsessions and compulsions. We will discuss some of the issues related to this problem in chapters 3 and 4. In this chapter, we want to focus on the obsessional syndrome and how it is related, and differentiated from, a number of other emotional conditions. We will focus on those conditions that present particular difficulty with respect to differentiation, on those about which there is a reasonable empirical literature, and on two conditions that provide some interesting psychopathological speculation.

ANXIETY

In the psychiatric nomenclature, *obsessive–compulsive disorder* is currently included under the category of anxiety disorders. From time to time there has been debate concerning just where this disorder belongs in the diagnostic schema. It should become clear why there has been some difference of opinion in this regard after our discussion of the relationship of OCD to various other conditions.

The anxiety disorders category basically consists of those disorders that were once labeled *neurotic*. In addition to OCD, using the current DSM-III-R system, these include the phobias, generalized anxiety disorder, panic disorder with and without agoraphobia, posttraumatic stress disorder, and a new category called *organic anxiety disorder*. This last condition is thought to result from a number of medical abnormalities.

All of these conditions have as their core the presence of maladaptive anxiety, and there is considerable overlap in symptoms. In fact, the recognition that these disorders share so many similarities has suggested to some that *neurosis* might be a better descriptive term. For example, Boyd et al. (1984) have shown that the presence of the symptom of one anxiety disorder increases the probability of the presence of symptoms of another. Barlow (1985) reported the existence of panic attacks in virtually all of the anxiety disorders including simple phobia. Generalized anxiety disorder, as defined by DSM-III, was not supposed to be characterized by panic attacks. This was clearly not the case, so in the DSM-III-R, a diagnosis of generalized anxiety disorder is permissible when panic attacks are present. Obsessional patients perform similarly to other anxiety patients on various psychometric instruments, although they tend to score more in the severe range (S. M. Turner et al., 1986). Finally, obsessive–compulsive patients respond favorably to the class of behavioral treatments used with other anxiety disorders.

In examining the specific symptom pattern of OCD and how it relates to other anxiety states, one finds remarkable overlap in the symptom picture. We have already indicated that it is not uncommon to see panic attacks in OCD; even when full-blown panic attacks are not present, there are frequently minipanic episodes. OCD patients, like other anxiety patients, typically spend a great deal of time worrying about their bodies and their various fears. The fear of panic in panic patients is much like the fear of losing control in obsessionals. In panic disorder, with and without agoraphobia, as well as in OCD, there is an attempt by the individual to neutralize or prevent the occurrence of some aversive event through the process of active or passive avoidance. Although OCD patients show the most prominent symptoms of obsessive doubting and compulsive ritualizing, similar behaviors can be seen in panic disorder with and without agoraphobia. For example, some agoraphobics repeatedly phone their spouses to assure themselves that all is well, and some agoraphobics travel only certain routes or when accompanied by certain individuals. These are clearly compulsive behaviors, even if the fears driving them are somewhat different from those seen in OCD. One can conclude from these examples that the behaviors of these various disorders, although different in topography, in many ways seem to be functionally equivalent. It is not our purpose here to argue that all of these conditions should be considered one basic disturbance; rather we have gone to considerable length to illustrate that OCD appears to be very similar to other anxiety states. Therefore, in our opinion, it is appropriately classed as an anxiety disorder.

Because there is so much overlap among the anxiety disorders, how does one differentiate OCD from other anxiety states? The primary consideration in making that determination is whether or not obsessive and compulsive symptoms predominate, as described in chapter 1. If this appears to be the primary symptom pattern, despite the presence of other anxiety symptoms, then a diagnosis of OCD is appropriate. Under the provisions of the latest Diagnostic and Statistical Manual, several other anxiety diagnoses can be given concurrently (American Psychiatric Association, 1987). In our opinion, there is considerable confusion regarding the diagnosis of anxiety disorders at the present. Much of this is related to the predominant role given to panic, a role that we believe is unjustified on the basis of the empirical evidence. A second problem is the rigid adherence to a categorical diagnostic system, when clearly there are dimensional aspects of many conditions. The primary point to remember is that OCD should be diagnosed on the basis of the clinical picture presented, and one should not be surprised to find symptoms of various other anxiety disorders in such cases.

PHOBIA

Phobias are included under the anxiety disorders category in the DSM-III-R. In a study conducted in our clinic (S. M. Turner et al., 1986), we concluded that this was an appropriate placement. However, we also noted that the fear and anxiety in phobic conditions tend to be less severe than in the anxiety states. In addition, fear tends to be more circumscribed in the phobic states. Various phobias are highly prevalent among OCD patients and those with other types of anxiety disorders. However, Rachman and Hodgson (1980) pointed out that there is a high degree of association between phobias and OCD. They argued that the most frequent characteristic of OCD patients is fear of dirt and disease and contamination, which leads to extensive avoidance behavior. When attempts at avoidance fail, escape behaviors designed to remove or reduce the danger signals emerge. The classic form of escape behavior in OCD is repetitive cleaning. Thus, repetitive cleaning can be seen as a natural consequence of a dirt–disease–contamination phobia. Following this line of reasoning, OCD can be viewed as a subclass of the larger category, *phobia*.

A number of studies appear to support this viewpoint. For example, Kringlen (1965) found that over half of his 91 OCD patients reported the presence of phobias. Rachman and Hodgson (1980) identified a number of common elements in OCD and phobias. *First*, both OCD and phobic patients respond to anxiety-eliciting stimuli (imagined or real) with increases in physiological arousal. *Second*, phobic and OCD stimuli result in increased subjective distress and discomfort. *Third*, both OCD and phobic responses almost invariably entail some form of avoidance behavior. Furthermore, both disorders show increased incidence of childhood fears and familial neuroses over "normals" (Lo, 1967; C. Rosenberg, 1967; Videbech, 1975).

Despite the close similarity between phobias and OCD, there are a number of important distinctions. *First*, the obsessional syndrome in OCD is characterized by continual preoccupation with disturbing and repetitive thoughts, which is not the case with focal phobias. Phobic patients show little distress when not in contact with the phobic stimulus. *Second*, obsessional states are characterized by a high level of general anxiety and dysphoric mood, a state that is not typical for phobic conditions. In general, the level of tension, self-doubt, ambivalence, and social disruption is less in phobic states. *Third*, the ritualistic behavior seen in OCD patients is frequently necessary despite lack of contact with the phobic stimuli. Finally, not all OCD patients suffer from a disease-and-contamination fear, although this is the largest single category. Based on these considerations, along with the vastly different treatment prognosis for OCD, we believe OCD is not simply a subclass of phobia and that these criteria are important for distinguishing between phobic states and OCD.

DEPRESSION

We noted in chapter 1 that OCD patients tend to be more severely depressed than those with any other anxiety disorders. Indeed, some investigators consider OCD to be an affective disorder rather than an anxiety disorder. The relationship of OCD to depression is a complex one. Thus, we will take some time to explore it in this chapter. The incidence of significant depression among OCD patients ranges from 17% to 35%

(Vaughan, 1976) to 66% (Solyom, Zamanyadek, Ledwick, & Kenny, 1971). Virtually all of our patients in one study showed significant depression, as measured by the Beck Depression Inventory (S. M. Turner et al., 1986). In most cases, depression in OCD appears to be a secondary symptom, appearing subsequent to the development of the obsessions and compulsions. This is borne out by a study conducted by Rachman and Hodgson (1980), who reported that 55% of their patients reported no depressive syndrome at the onset of the OCD symptoms. However, numerous patients reported the development of depressive symptoms later on. Welner and Horowitz (1976) noted that depression was three times more likely to follow the onset of OCD than to precede it. It should be pointed out however, that exacerbation of one tends to cause worsening of the other, which can then result in the establishment of a vicious cycle. Present diagnostic practice allows for the diagnosis of major depression and OCD simultaneously. However, the primary disorder is usually considered the disorder that appeared first.

The relationship of anxiety to depression in general has generated considerable debate. There are those who view anxiety as a manifestation of an affective state. Yet, there is mounting evidence that the two syndromes, despite considerable overlap, have important differences in symptoms, course, and prognostic picture. For example, in the series of studies comprising the Newcastle Studies, Roth and Mountjoy (1982) concluded that, despite much overlap, depression was characterized by a group of symptoms statistically different from those occurring in anxiety. Recently, Kendler, Heath, Martin, and Eaves (1987), using multivariative procedures, found different core characteristics for anxiety and depression. In addition, the prognosis for recovery from depression is much better than for anxiety. Similarly, the family history, clinical course, and mortality for anxiety patients can be clearly distinguished from a matched group of depressed patients (Coryell, 1981).

All of these parameters seem to differentiate OCD from depressive disorders, as they do the other anxiety states. It has been our practice to consider OCD the primary disorder if it occurred first, regardless of how severe the depression might be. Depression, however, becomes a major issue with respect to treatment, and this will be discussed in subsequent chapters.

SCHIZOPHRENIA

Speculation concerning the relationship of OCD and schizophrenia has existed for some time. However, this notion is not given much credence by current investigators. Black (1974) examined the incidence of OCD patients who subsequently developed schizophrenia and reported probabilities of OCD patients developing schizophrenia ranging from 0.0% to 3.3%, based on a sample of over 300 patients. Similarly, Lo (1967) found only 2 out of 88 OCD patients who subsequently developed a schizophrenic disorder. Recently, Rachman and Hodgson (1980) reported that none of 83 OCD patients treated in a series of studies went on to develop a schizophrenic condition. However, Insel and Akiskal (1986) reported a number of "psychotic-like" features in obsessional states and noted that these features appeared to be on a continuum of severity between OCD and psychosis. Of course, this can be said for a number of conditions, including normality. Nevertheless, the presence of a number of features to be discussed in the section on personality disorders in this chapter, such as those reported by Insel and Akiskal (1986), and the presence of *overvalued ideation* in OCD continue to fuel speculation of a possible link with psychosis.

With respect to overvalued ideation, we note in chapter 4 that this behavior has considerable importance for treatment and prognosis. One of the cardinal features of OCD is the patients' recognition of the senselessness of their actions. Thus, OCD patients complain that they know that their behavior is irrational but that they are unable to prevent themselves from engaging in it due to uncontrollable urges. However, there is a small number of patients who do not view their behavior as senseless or irrational but rather believe that they have sufficient cause for their concern and that their rituals will prevent the occurrence of disastrous consequences (we discuss such a case in chapter 4). In every other way, these patients meet the criteria for OCD and typically are given this diagnosis. Foa (1979) noted that these patients do not respond as well to behavioral treatment, and this is consistent with our own clinical experience. The important element in overvalued ideation is not the content but the individuals' belief in the validity of their fear.

Obsessional patients show varying degrees of certainty about the rationality or irrationality of their beliefs. However, most do acknowledge that their fears are senseless. With respect to that class of patients seen as having overvalued ideation, the degree of rigidity with respect to the belief varies, but they never acknowledge that it is senseless. In its severest form, this type of ideation is as firmly held as any delusion usually associated with a psychosis, and it might well be considered a monosymptomatic delusion. However, these patients do not show other signs of psychosis. Further investigation will need to be conducted to clarify this construct.

Although delusions of schizophrenics can sometimes resemble obsessions, such as somatic concerns and fears of bodily infestation (Munro, 1980), and schizophrenics sometimes engage in ritualistic behavior, it is usually easy to distinguish between the two conditions. Obsessive patients do not have positive symptoms of schizophrenia such as halluci- nations and formal thought disorders. Obsessionals typically recognize the irrationality of their behavior, whereas schizophrenics do not. Rituals seen in schizophrenia do not appear to have a purpose, or they are in response to some type of "instructions" received from external forces. On the other hand, the rituals of obsessionals clearly serve a specified func- tion. Finally, obsessionals do not experience the feeling of being controlled or directed by external forces, and their interpersonal difficulties are not fueled by the suspicion and distrust characteristic of schizophrenia.

PERSONALITY DISORDERS

As in any other disorder, the patient with OCD exhibits a variety of pathological personality attributes. Thus, one can see an OCD patient, for example, with the cluster of symptoms comprising the diagnostic category of obsessive–compulsive personality disorder or with the characteristics of a dependent personality disorder. Alternatively, a patient might not meet the formal criteria for any of the personality disorders defined in DSM-III- R. The existence of these various conditions is important because, in our experience, they do have relevance for the management of the OCD patient and could have relevance for treatment effectiveness and long- term maintenance. A recent report by Mavissakalian and Hammen (1987) indicated that personality characteristics are important predictors of treat- ment outcome with agoraphobia.

At one time, it was assumed that the onset of OCD was always preceded by the presence of an obsessive–compulsive personality disturbance. As defined in DSM-III-R, this condition is characterized by the following: (a) being serious, conventional and stingy, with restricted ability to express warm emotions; (b) being perfectionistic and overly concerned with details at the expense of the big picture; (c) insisting that others submit to one's way of doing things, without showing concern for the feelings of others; (d) showing excessive involvement with work at the expense of pleasure and interpersonal relationships; and (e) being indecisive, being tardy, and procrastinating. For a diagnosis, four of these five qualities must be pre- sent.

It has become clear in recent years that this personality picture is not always present in patients with OCD. Slade (1974) concluded that evidence for the existence of an obsessional personality disorder differs, depending upon whether psychometric studies or clinical studies are used. Clinical studies tend to suggest a much stronger relationship than do psychometric studies. Even though formal criteria for obsessive–compulsive personality might not be met, clearly the vast majority of patients seen in our clinic exhibit some of those features in varying degrees of severity. The lack of

TOCD C

clarity regarding the entire domain of personality disorders makes it difficult to discuss fully or assess what the relationship of OCD to these characteristics really is. Thus, the disorder is diagnosed whether or not there is a concurrent obsessive–compulsive personality disorder.

Recently, there has been considerable discussion about the possibility of a subset of obsessional patients who might have at least some psychotic features. Furthermore, it has been suggested that these individuals make up the group of patients who have been most resistent to current behavioral and pharmacologic treatments (Jenike, Baer, Minichiello, Schwartz, & Carey, 1986). Some of this concern has been focused on schizotypal personality disorder, a disorder characterized by many features similar to schizophrenia but much less severe. Individuals with this condition can have periods where they appear frankly psychotic, usually in response to severe stress. We have treated a number of OCD patients with schizotypal personality features and agree that the treatment process is more difficult and does not appear to be as effective, and maintenance of treatment gains is problematic. The presence of a schizotypal personality disorder does not preclude the diagnosis of OCD, but we believe further research will demonstrate that this is a poor prognostic sign and refinement of the current treatment approach may be necessary for this group.

OTHER CONDITIONS

Obsessional behavior and rituals can be seen in a number of disorders. For example, obsessive–compulsive symptoms can occur during recovery from head injury (McKeon, McGuffin, & Robinson, 1984). In such cases, the symptoms can persist for many years, even after normalizing of neurological functioning. It is unclear if these patients had OCD features prior to their injuries. Jenike and Brotman (1984) reported electroencephalogram-abnormalities in 4 of 12 obsessional patients. The abnormality was suggestive of temporal lobe abnormality. However, it was not clear whether the OCD was in any way related to the EEG abnormality. A host of biological parameters have been identified as being associated with OCD (Turner, Beidel, & Nathan, 1985). Yet assessment would not be conducted on a routine basis but rather when clinical considerations dictate. One indication for a more comprehensive evaluation of physical status might be the onset of OCD above the age of 35, because the majority of the anxiety disorders develop prior to that age.

An association of OCD with Tourette's syndrome, a movement disorder characterized by involuntary repetitive movement and tics, has been suggested. The disorders are known to occur simultaneously in some instances, and a pathophysiological link has been suggested (Pauls,

Toubin, Leckman, Zahner, & Cohen, 1986). Tourette's patients frequently have obsessions and also display behaviors that seem to resemble compulsive rituals. Similarly, OCD patients sometimes exhibit a variety of tic-like behaviors. Over the past few years, we have seen only a few patients who had both conditions. Similarly, Rasmussen and Tsuang (1986) reported only 2 patients out of their sample of 44 patients who had both disorders. At this point, there appears to be little justification for group; ng these two conditions together. When both conditions are present, both should be diagnosed.

Dysmorphophobia is grouped under somatoform disorders in DSM-III-R. This disorder is characterized by an inordinate preoccupation with some imagined defect in physical apperance. As an example, we were involved in the treatment of a female patient who was preoccupied with the size of her breasts. After numerous surgical procedures to increase and decrease the size, she was referred for evaluation by her plastic surgeon. DSM-III-R notes that depressive features and obsessive–compulsive personality traits are common characteristics of dysmorphophobics' condition (p. 256).

We have been struck by the obsessional features of these patients. In fact, there appears to be little difference between the two disorders, except that dysmorphophobics tend to be concerned with a particular part of the body, usually the facial area or the breast. Also, it is not uncommon to see dysmorphophobic features in patients who have a more pervasive obsessive–compulsive syndrome. The prevalence of this condition was once thought to be very small. However, DSM-III-R points out that recent evidence suggests that it is more prevalent than previously considered. Many of these patients are seeing various medical specialists such as plastic surgeons and might not be referred for psychiatric evaluation. Although there are few data available, we believe there is cause to further examine the relationship of these patients to obsessionals. In the cases that we have been involved with, similar treatment strategies have been employed, with some positive results.

Bulimia (bulimia nervosa in DSM-III-R) is another condition with obsessional characteristics. The disorder is defined by recurrent episodes of binge eating, a feeling of lack of control over eating, self-induced vomiting, use of laxatives or diuretics, strict fasting or vigorous exercise, and overconcern with weight and body size (DSM-III-R, p. 67). Many of the characteristics of this disorder are strikingly similar to obsessive–compulsive disorder, differing mainly in the topography of the behavior. Furthermore, it should be pointed out that OCD patients frequently report histories of binge eating, are often concerned with body functioning, and sometimes engage in ritualistic exercise programs. Similar also is the presence of an intense urge; in the case of the bulimic, an urge to eat. Moreover, engaging in the eating behavior results in temporary drive reduction.

Currently, the three disorders discussed in this section can be diagnosed concurrently with obsessive–compulsive disorder. We have discussed them here for differential diagnostic considerations and because they present interesting and challenging questions regarding their psychopathology and their place in the classification system.

SUMMARY

We have discussed the primary questions regarding the differentiation of obsessive–compulsive disorder from a number of conditions. Despite arguments about the classification of OCD, the disorder is similar to, and shares many features with, other anxiety disorders. Its relationship to depression is much more complex, although anxiety states can be differentiated from depressive states. The role of obsessive–compulsive personality traits in the disorder is unclear, as are features of other personality disturbances, but most obsessionals do show some of the features comprising the syndrome of obsessive–compulsive personality disorder. Finally, several conditions currently not considered as OCD share many of the core features of the disorder, and the nature of their relationship to OCD deserves further study.

Chapter 3
Assessment and Patient Management

The initial contact between the obsessional patient and the therapist can be a trying experience for both. The obsessional patient is often ambivalent about the whole affair, is often reluctant to discuss all aspects of the problem, is frequently concerned about being viewed as "crazy", and, in many instances, feels that no intervention will be able to help. Although these issues can be associated with any disorder, they appear to be particularly relevant for obsessionals and often present a formidable challenge to the therapist during assessment. In this chapter, we will focus on some of the important assessment issues related to obsessive–compulsives, provide some suggestions for how they might be handled, and discuss various types of assessment strategies that might be used.

The initial meeting should undoubtedly be centered around information gathering. At the heart of the first session, and possibly several subsequent ones, is clinical assessment. In conducting the assessment, there are numerous modalities the therapist can employ, including clinical interviewing, self-report inventories, behavioral self-monitoring, psychophysiological assessment, biological and physical assessments, and neurophysiological or neuropsychological testing. In addition to evaluating the obsessions and compulsions, the clinician needs to assess for the presence of other behaviors viewed as personality attributes and commonly encountered in obsessive–compulsive patients, such as anger, hostility, rigidity, and control. The existence of these characteristics might affect the assessment process, how treatment is conceptualized and implemented, and how effective treatment ultimately will be. Therefore, in addition to presenting strategies useful in assessing the symptom pattern of obsessive–compulsive disorder, we will discuss in this chapter a set of clinical strategies that could be even more important: procedures needed to effectively manage the behavior of patients with obsessive–compulsive disorder. These strategies are considered essential, in that appropriate management greatly enhances the clinician's effectiveness in treating the primary disorder.

One of the more important characteristics of OCD patients that is critical for the assessment period is their secretive natures. These patients often go to great lengths to prevent detection of their obsessions and rituals by even the closest family members. For example, one patient related to us that she would get up in the middle of the night to wash her children's building blocks, in order to avoid observation by family members. This secrecy could be apparent in some initial degree of reluctance to discuss symptoms with the clinician. This reluctance could stem from several different sources, including the horrific nature of some thoughts and images and the belief that others will perceive the obsessional thoughts as stupid, unworthy of attention, or within control if only the patients would "try hard enough". However, patients with intrusive images such as stabbing their parents with knives or strangling their children as they sleep might initially be hesitant to reveal the existence of these socially unacceptable thoughts and images to a stranger. In addition to the culturally unacceptable nature of these images, patients might have tried very hard to suppress them and, by discussing them, might feel that in some way they could lose control and come closer to acting them out. We have found it useful to guide patients through this by asking if they have experienced various types of obsessions or rituals. They are often surprised that we would know to ask such questions, and this often helps them feel more at ease.

A second source of reluctance can be a prior history of punishment by others when these fears were disclosed. Patients who have contamination fears, for example, might have related their concerns to spouses or close family members, who probably reacted with incredulity. As another example, in the movie *The Four Seasons*, an actor who reveals his most intimate fear, a fear of elastic, is greeted with uproarious laughter by his friends. Many obsessive–compulsive patients have had similar experiences.

The therapist should consider the possibility of reluctance when, during the course of the interview, the patient lists a vague series of ills including somatic complaints, worrying, and other nonspecific concerns. The therapist initially should allow the patient to set the pace of the interview, following up with more specific questions and inquiring about the meaning of phrases such as "when something happens." The clinician should not react with surprise or revulsion to any obsessions or compulsions (e.g., horrific images) described by the patient. Although this might seem to be an elementary point, graphic details of twisting knives in someone's eyes could engender such responses. Therefore, when listening to descriptions of these images, the therapist should be extremely cautious about all aspects of her or his behavior, particularly slight changes in facial expression. A straightforward and direct demeanor often serves to reduce patient concern. Reassuring statements that the clinician has heard many unusual thoughts and behaviors can serve to reduce the patient's anxiety about this issue. In particular, questions about the experience of various types of obsessions and compulsions demonstrate to the patient that the therapist understands the disorder. The patients are frequently surprised that the therapist can anticipate some of his or her problem areas and that other persons have reported the same or similar problems.

A third important problem often encountered by clinicians is ambivalence about entering treatment. An obvious example of ambivalence is the patient who attempts to bargain with the therapist by setting limits on what constitutes appropriate behaviors for intervention. A patient might state that she or he would like to get rid of some rituals but keep others or might proclaim that she or he does not believe there is any way to treat or eliminate certain obsessions and rituals. Although the patient is certainly often able to relate which of the obsessions and compulsions appear to be the most problematic and which are not, it is our policy to convey to the patient early on that we must have the latitude to decide on the pace, scope, and type of treatment that is needed. We explain to the patient that "partial treatment" usually results in minimal improvement and subsequent relapse. The patient is informed that the nature of the treatment is such that he or she will need to be fully committed to receive any benefit, and, although we discuss in detail any intervention before we begin, we will not enter into negotiations with the patient. In addition, it is our policy that the clinician, after reviewing the assessment data with the patient, decides which behaviors are targeted for intervention. If the therapist senses ambivalence, the patient is asked to take some time to consider whether or not she or he is willing to undergo such a time-consuming treatment program at the time. This tough stance is taken because compromise in many instances renders treatment ineffective, and the struggle over control can develop into a constant issue unless effectively managed initially.

The clinician often encounters a patient who is hostile. This behavior is displayed directly or indirectly. For example, the patient might question the therapist's credentials, age, or ability to carry out the treatment intervention. The patient might express doubt that the clinician "really" understands the nature or extent of the patient's difficulties. The patient might also reveal overtly hostile or passive–aggressive actions directed toward other individuals, as well as toward the therapist.

Hostility can sometimes be the result of heightened anxiety. In individuals without OCD, environmental stressors are often associated with increased incidents of angry outbursts. Thus, it is not surprising that obsessive–compulsives, who might exist for long periods of time in highly anxious states, can manifest a great deal of hostility. Hostile personal attacks directed by patients at therapists can be addressed by (a) acknowledging that high levels of anxiety can make individuals hostile or angry or (b) remaining unmoved and ignoring the attack. Our usual approach is to confront such behavior in a direct fashion and use this episode to determine if this is a characteristic mode of responding, particularly when under stress. Hostility directed toward people responsible for increased anxiety (in this case, the therapist) is not unexpected. One patient who was undergoing in vivo flooding for fears related to various cleaning agents engaged in numerous maneuvers to ensure that the therapist got the material on him as well. Direct confrontation regarding this matter revealed that the patient felt degraded by having to engage in this behavior. This passive–aggressive style was also found to be a characteristic way that this person handled interpersonal stress. If it is determined that such behavior is a general characteristic, it should be dealt with directly during the maintenance phase of treatment, which is discussed in chapter 6. Patients should be reminded that, if there is dissatisfaction with the therapist or the procedures, they should feel free to raise the issue. Although we are careful to explain to patients the nature of the disorder and to provide a general description of the treatment and what can be expected, we stress that the patients must decide if treatment is what they want. Very few patients choose not to enter treatment or to discontinue therapy before completion.

Patients with OCD can also be quite manipulative. Many have managed to coerce family members into respecting or overtly participating in their rituals. It is quite common for patients to require that family members engage in various behaviors to satisfy their needs. One example of this is a patient recently treated in our clinic who required all family members to remove their clothing and shower in the basement before entering the home. One patient with obsessional worries about injuring someone in an automobile accident had several family members monitor different newscasts each evening to be reassured that no hit-and-run accidents had occurred that day.

Given the opportunity, patients will manipulate therapists as well. For example, on one occasion, when a therapist was to take a patient on an outdoor flooding session, the clinician walked through the building to the outside, through three sets of doors, always with the patient lagging behind. Only later did the therapist realize that the patient's lagging behind was deliberate, designed to avoid touching doors and doorknobs by having the therapist engage in the behavior. Manipulative behavior is probably the most difficult patient characteristic for the novice therapist to immediately recognize and respond to appropriately. However, if the therapist observes patient behaviors that are unusual in any way (an obvious example is pushing elevator buttons or opening doors with the elbows rather than the hands), the motivation for the behavior should be questioned. Most patients will respond truthfully by stating that it is due to some obsession or constitutes a compulsion. Clinical judgment is necessary at this point to determine if the patients were really being manipulative or if the avoidance pattern is so ingrained that they honestly forgot the behavior's original purpose (e.g., avoidance). We have found that most cases are usually deliberate manipulation. However, there have been some instances where questioning has resulted in a genuine expression of surprise on the part of patients and admission that they had forgotten about the particular reason for the behavior. Once manipulation is recognized, patients should be told that exposure therapy, for example, involves direct contact with the stimulus. Deliberate attempts to manipulate the therapist or to avoid exposure only defeat the purpose of the sessions and therefore must be discontinued. Therapists must stand firm on this issue, although there will be, in all probability, further attempts by patients to bargain with or manipulate the treatment.

Manipulative behavior is particularly difficult to control when more than one therapist is involved in assessment and treatment. As an example, one very manipulative patient, treated on an inpatient basis, was given specific instructions to conduct further exposure sessions on the unit. The patient, however, disliked the instructions and convinced another staff member that his treatment plan would be better served if he left the unit for several hours. This type of behavior will occur despite the most detailed explanations of treatment. In fact, inpatients are routinely given a copy of their detailed treatment plans. Nevertheless, behavior such as that described is not uncommon. If such behavior persists, patients are warned that future occurrences will result in discharge and termination of our involvement in their treatment.

In summary, there are several behavioral styles common to obsessive–compulsive patients that present management issues for therapists assessing and treating individuals with this disorder. Most require a calm, professional demeanor and the ability to stand firm in the face of hostility, manipulation, and reluctance. Clinicians must be firm but, at the same time, convey a sense of caring and understanding of the patients' condition. Clinicians who can accomplish this will find their effectiveness with obsessive–compulsive patients vastly enhanced.

ASSESSMENT STRATEGIES

The Clinical Interview

The usual point of departure for assessment of OCD is a face-to-face interview. The advantage of an interview format is that it does not require any special equipment. The disadvantage is that interviewing for obsessive–compulsive symptoms does require specialized clinical expertise if reliable and valid information is to be obtained. The importance of the interview cannot be overemphasized; in addition to gathering information about specific dysfunctional behaviors, the interview has two additional purposes: to elucidate patient characteristics that could affect the validity of the assessment or impede the progress of treatment (e.g., hostile, dependent, or defensive behavior) and to set the tone for future therapist–patient interactions. The salient patient characteristics have been discussed earlier in this chapter and in chapters 1 and 2. In this section, we will discuss issues of assessment specific to the clinical interview.

The primary goal of the interview is to delineate the patient's specific obsessions and compulsions and to understand the complete clinical picture. The manner in which the questions are phrased could affect the information that is elicited. Given the secretive nature of the OCD patient, the clinician who poses questions such as "Do you have any washing rituals?" might not uncover ritualistic behaviors. A case referred to us for consultation, which was described as a "thunderstorm phobic", will serve to illustrate this point. During a routine initial interview, this man denied any other fears or worries or any ritualistic behaviors. Upon deciding to use an imaginal flooding paradigm to address his fear, we asked him, during a more detailed assessment, to describe how he felt and what he did during a thunderstorm. When questioned in this fashion, the patient revealed an entire set of intricate rituals conducted during the thunderstorm. These included standing out in the rain with a flashlight to monitor a small stream near his home, ritualistic checking of all the windows in the house in a specific fashion, and compulsive monitoring of the weather channel for the existence of future thunderstorms. Without conducting this detailed inquiry, we would not have discovered the existence of these rituals and would have neglected a significant aspect of this patient's disorder.

When assessing for obsessions and compulsions, it is important to collect information on both the duration and frequency of each specific behavior. To offer a simplistic example, if a patient is asked how many times he or she washes his or her hands per day, the patient might reply "only nine or ten." If the clinician does not follow this with a question about the duration of each hand washing, the information that each washing ritual lasts for 1 hour could be missed. In addition, there is a possibility that the phrasing of the question in the manner of "Do you have any washing rituals?" might not elicit the information that the patient uses an ammonia-based household cleaner to wash hands and hair. Without therapist knowledge of the use of this cleaner, the patient might follow instructions to decrease both the time and number of washing, but might not stop using the cleaner. Therefore, treatment would only be partially effective. To gain maximum benefit from the interview data, the therapist should use open-ended questions such as "Describe exactly what you do when you begin to take your shower." Giving the patient the opportunity to describe the rituals provides the therapist with detailed information concerning all of the behaviors that need to be addressed during treatment and also allows the therapist to pose questions that elicit information that is not provided. It should also be pointed out here that the frequency and duration parameters might also be important in assessing treatment outcome. A patient could show considerable improvement in the frequency of a behavior but not the duration. Obviously, both parameters must improve before treatment is terminated.

It would be highly unusual for patients to describe all of the symptoms during one assessment session. This should not necessarily be construed as holding out on their part. Individuals with severe obsessive–compulsive disorder have such a myriad of extensive and intricate rituals that it is likely that some behaviors will not be immediately apparent. During assessment and treatment, the therapist should continue informal assessment to detect the emergence of additional obsessions and compulsions.

Sometimes ritualistic behaviors are carried out during the assessment session. For example, patients who feel compelled to "check" items or places might attempt to do so in front of their therapists during the sessions. Patients also repeatedly question their therapists about issues that had previously been discussed. In managing these behaviors, therapists should first point out the compulsive nature of the behavior to the patients, that is, the fact that the question has been previously addressed. In the instance of repeated questioning, further questions for the same information should be ignored, or therapists might wish to simply say, "I will not answer that question again." Other compulsive behaviors during assessment should be treated in an identical fashion, that is, by instructing patients to immediately discontinue the behavior.

The Role of Family Members

The initial assessment of obsessions and compulsions would be incomplete without assessing the role of family members. As noted earlier, families are often participants in rituals. A family member might be required to act as a chauffeur for an obsessive–compulsive patient who refuses to drive due to fears of injuring someone with an automobile. Family participation might be more extensive, as in the case of one patient who was so fearful that her kitchen might be contaminated by food particles that she insisted all food preparation and meal consumption be done in the basement. Appliances, a dinette table and chairs, and all groceries were kept in the basement as well. An assessment of family involvement is important for adequate treatment planning, particularly when home-response prevention is part of the treatment protocol. The relationship with family members often figures prominently in referral for treatment, and often the behavior of family members needs to be managed in some fashion. Thus, in both instances cited, meetings had to be held with family members to discuss their role in helping to maintain the disorder and the changes that would be necessary for treatment to be effective.

Other Clinical Issues

In addition to assessing for obsessions and compulsions, the therapist also should assess other aspects of the patient's mental status. In particular, depressive symptoms should be adequately addressed because they can have particular relevance to how treatment is conducted and to subsequent outcome. Behaviors such as sleep and appetite disturbance should be noted, and, if severe, the clinician should consider the use of psychotropic medication to ameliorate depressive symptoms. Suicidal ideation, other anxiety disorders, and the incidence of psychotic symptoms should also be noted.

When the information-gathering phase of the interview has been completed, it is incumbent upon the clinician to provide some information about the disorder to the patient. For example, the majority of patients admitted to our Anxiety Disorders Clinic enter with a long history of failed treatment interventions. They often wonder if this will be another treatment that will also be unsuccessful. Although seeking relief from their symptoms, they have often had the disorder for a long period of time and feel somewhat hopeless. At this point, the patient does not need platitudes and false promises but requires realistic information concerning treatment efficacy. The patient should be told that there are interventions available to reduce, and possibly eliminate, the obsessions and compulsions, but that there is no instantaneous cure. Treatment for obsessive–compulsive disorder is a long-term process that requires commitment and active participation on the part of the patient.

In addition to information on treatment efficacy, patients also need realistic information on the nature of OCD and what the treatment process will entail. Concerning the nature of obsessive–compulsive disorder, patients should be told that it is a chronic disorder they could experience to some degree for the rest of their lives. Although interventions are available to reduce or eliminate the frequency of obsessions and compulsions, some patients might always experience residual anxiety or at least be likely to experience episodes of high anxiety on a periodic basis. Patients should understand that the disorder can be exacerbated by stress and that reoccurrence of symptoms can be expected with future stressful events. Information of this type gives patients a realistic outlook on their disorder, impresses upon them the severity of their condition, and yet offers hope for the remediation of their most distressful symptoms.

As noted, patients with OCD also need realistic information about the nature of the treatment interventions. If medication is to be a part of the treatment plan, patients should be told about the drug and its effects and possible side effects. Likewise, behavioral interventions should be explained. Patients should be told that treatment will involve helping them to face the objects or situations they currently fear and that they will be given instructions in how to avoid or prevent engagement in the rituals. Although patients often press for more details regarding the nature of the behavioral intervention, we have found that it is counterproductive to provide too many details of the treatment intervention at the assessment phase. We have found that premature explanations of exposure strategies provide more material for the obsessional and only raise objections on the part of patients that they have tried to stop but that it does not work. Also, many details sometimes increase apprehensiveness. Our response to patients who press for details of the behavioral intervention is to respond that we prefer not to provide premature explanations and that information will be provided at treatment onset. Patients who will be undergoing flooding and response prevention should be told that it is an intensive intervention procedure, that sessions will be conducted often for the first few weeks, and that each treatment session could last several hours.

In summary, the clinical interview is the initial point for assessment of the range and severity of the patient's obsessive–compulsive symptoms. When conducted by a skilled clinician, the interview can provide an extensive overall picture of the patient's clinical state. Additionally, the interview can form the basis of a sound therapeutic relationship and be useful in identifying patient characteristics that could have an effect on

assessment and treatment. Institution of appropriate patient management procedures from the outset of the interview will establish the
behaviors to be expected by the patient and therapist throughout the
duration of assessment and treatment.

Self-Report Inventories

Various self-report inventories can be useful in helping the therapist
understand the patient's overall condition, and they might also be useful
as indications of improvement. There are several instruments that have
been used extensively to both assess symptomatology and evaluate
treatment outcome. It should be noted that these inventories were not
designed to diagnose obsessive–compulsive disorder (Hodgson &
Rachman, 1977) but to provide information on variables such as severity,
functional impairment, and specific ritualistic behaviors.

One of the most frequently cited instruments, the Maudsley Obsessional–Compulsive Inventory is a 30-item self-report inventory for assessing various types of obsessive–compulsive complaints (Hodgson &
Rachman, 1977). This instrument, in addition to providing a gross overall
score, contains subscales for assessment of four types of obsessive–compulsive behaviors: checking, cleaning, slowness, and doubting. As noted
by the authors, the scale was not designed to cover the entire range of
obsessional problems but only those associated with observable rituals.
Thus, the items on the inventory reflect common ritualistic behaviors and
thinking styles, with little or no attention to the content of obsessional
thoughts and images. In addition, the inventory was not designed to
assess obsessional personality traits. Items were chosen specifically for
their ability to differentiate obsessional patients from other "neurotic"
patients, resulting in a scale geared specifically to assessment of obsessive–compulsive behaviours. The instrument possesses good test-retest
reliability ($r = .89$; Rachman & Hodgson, 1980).

In the initial publication (Hodgson & Rachman, 1977), the checking,
cleaning, and total obsessional scores were validated on a sample of
patients with obsessive–compulsive disorder. A later study, using a
college student sample (Rachman & Hodgson, 1980), provided further
confirmation of the checking and cleaning components and a doubting–
conscientiousness factor. Replication using a sample of Italian university
students also validated the checking, cleaning, and doubting scales and
provided some evidence of a slowness factor (Sanavio & Vidotto, 1985).

The Maudsley Obsessional–Compulsive Inventory is easy to administer-
ter and score. Only 30 items in length, it appears to provide reliable and
valid data on the existence of several types of obsessive–compulsive
behaviors. The disadvantages lie in its use of a true-and-false format and

its limitation to an assessment of mainly ritualistic behaviors. Use of a true-and-false format provides for the endorsement of a particular behavior, but it does not allow for measurement of severity. Given the chronic nature of obsessive–compulsive disorder, severity would seem to be an important dimension, particularly when assessing treatment outcome. That is, after intervention, rituals and worrying might be greatly reduced but not eliminated. Positive changes would be less apparent using a dichotomous response format than a Likert-scale. The second disadvantage, as noted, is the scale's limitation to ritualistic behaviors. The nature and content of obsessional thinking cannot be assessed directly with the use of this inventory. It should be noted, however, that the scale was developed deliberately to differentiate obsessive–compulsive patients from other neurotic patients who also sometimes manifest obsessional styles. Thus, in the Maudsley Obsessional–Compulsive Inventory, comprehensiveness is secondary to discriminative accuracy.

Another self-report inventory, The Leyton Obsessional Inventory (Cooper, 1970) is a 60–item self-report instrument designed to assess obsessional symptoms and obsessional traits. The original format of the Leyton utilized a card-sort procedure, but a more recent version uses the standard paper-and-pencil format (Snowdon, 1980). The Leyton Obsessional Inventory contains two types of questions, the first 46 being symptom questions and the latter 21 being trait questions. This latter group includes behaviors such as moodiness, meanness, irritability, hoarding, punctuality, and stubbornness (Cooper & Kelleher, 1973). Cooper (1970) theorized that this second group of behaviors were common in individuals who developed obsessive–compulsive disorder. Thus, the Leyton Obsessional Inventory differs from the Maudsley Obsessional–Compulsive Inventory by its inclusion of personality characteristics that could be related to but are not necessarily specific to obsessive–compulsive disorder.

The Leyton Obsessional Inventory also differs from the Maudsley instrument in its response format. Questions on the Leyton Obsessional Inventory are phrased so as to be answered yes or no. For those questions that are answered affirmatively, further information is requested: the degree to which the individual views the behavior as nonsensical and the degree of functional impairment created by the thoughts and behavior. The degree of resistance is rated on a 5-point scale, whereas the dysfunction rating uses a 4-point scale. Thus, this inventory incorporates the patient's estimate of severity and incidence and can provide scores for symptoms, traits, resistance, and interference. The Leyton Obsessional Inventory is capable of differentiating obsessional patients from a group of normal controls and, like the Maudsley Obsessional–Compulsive Inventory, has been analyzed with principal-component and factor-analytic procedures (Cooper & Kelleher, 1973). The results, based on a sample of normal adults, revealed three distinct components: cleanliness, checking, and incompleteness. The third component was composed of questions about doubting and uncertainty. These three components are virtually identical to those comprising the Maudsley instrument.

With respect to its psychometric properties, the Leyton Obsessional Inventory appears to have acceptable concurrent and discriminant capabilities. The instrument was significantly correlated with patient and assessor ratings of severity ($r = .61$ to $.81$); Fear Thermometer ratings ($r = .47$); avoidance tasks ($r = .52$); and scores on semantic differential scales ($r = .53$ to $.73$) (Rachman, Marks, & Hodgson, 1973). Scores on the inventory are also capable of differentiating obsessive–compulsive patients from a group of normal controls. Patients score significantly higher on the trait, symptoms, resistance, and interference subscales. The advantages of the Leyton Obsessional Inventory include its more comprehensive item pool, assessment of degree of impairment, and use of rating scales to determine severity.

Although, the Leyton instrument is still in need of empirical investigation, it is likely that it possesses greater utility in assessing treatment outcome, given this greater latitude by which to assess change. However, for some patients, the number of choices that are required could be a disadvantage. Particularly for those patients who are extremely indecisive, the Leyton Obsessional Inventory could present an overwhelming challenge. For example, many of our patients have a great deal of difficulty with simple, forced choice responses, being unable to decide "true" or "false." The Leyton, with its necessity to cover the same material possibly several times and make even finer distinctions might prove too overwhelming, causing the patient to get stuck or give up. Scoring the inventory is also more difficult but, as noted, does provide a finer grained analysis of the patient's clinical state.

Partially in response to the length and complexity of the Leyton Obsessional Inventory, Allen and Tune (1975) developed the Lynfield Obsessional/Compulsive Questionnaire(s). The questionnaire is composed of 20 items taken directly from the Leyton Obsessional Inventory. Eleven questions are the full set of items that make up the three principal components of the Leyton (cleanliness, checking, and incompleteness). Nine additional items were drawn from the Leyton to widen the range of symptomatology to be assessed, and these address the area of rumination. The format was converted from a card-sort to a paper-and-pencil procedure. The 20 questions are printed on two forms; one for the endorsement of resistance and the other for the endorsement of interference responses. One drawback of the Lynfield instruments is that other diagnostic groups who also have obsessional symptoms (e.g., schizophrenics) score as high as patients with obsessive–compulsive disorder (Allen & Tune, 1975). Thus, the authors have noted that the short questionnaires should be used to measure obsessional symptoms, not as a tool to diagnose obsessive–compulsive disorder.

The research literature also contains reference to several other self-report measures including the Sandler and Hazari Obsessionality Scale (Sandler & Hazari, 1960), the Hysteroid/Obsessoid Questionnaire (Foulds, 1965; Foulds & Caine, 1958, 1959), and the Obsessive-Compulsive Checklist (Philpott, 1975). As is the case with the Lynfield Questionnaires, there are few reports on the psychometric properties of these instruments, and they have not been widely adopted for use in clinical or research settings (S. M. Turner & Michelson, 1984).

In summary, self-report inventories are useful in helping to gather information on the entire range of dysfunctional behavior and therefore could assist in conducting a more comprehensive assessment than interviewing alone. In addition, improvement on these instruments may be used to objectify the assessment of treatment outcome. The admonition that the inventory be used to measure symptom severity, and not to make a diagnosis, should be adopted by assessors as a general guideline. *First*, it is poor clinical practice to rely on a self-report instrument for diagnosis. *Second*, each of these inventories has a number of components, and an individual with severe behavior dysfunction limited to one of the components would not necessarily have a high total score on any of the inventories. Although the majority of patients have some degree of both washing and checking behaviors, it is also true that most patients can be described as primarily washers, checkers, or cognitive ritualizers. Thus, a simple tally of items scored in the dysfunctional direction might not fully assess the degree of impairment and severity. Self-report instruments should be given to the patients to complete, be reviewed by the therapist to discover any behaviors not previously reported, and be used for further interview or assessment if necessary.

Behavioral Self-Monitoring

Mischel (1972) wrote that the best method by which to understand something about a person was to ask the person directly. Simple, direct methods of assessment appear to prove as accurate, if not more so, as more elaborate indirect assessment strategies. Both interviewing and self-report inventories fall into the category of direct-measurement procedures, and both can help provide an overall picture of the patient's clinical state. However, given the anxious and impaired state of some obsessive–compulsive patients, the clinician might wish to obtain more detailed information by asking the patient to keep a daily record of obsessions and compulsions. The recording of the frequency of obsessional thoughts and ritualistic behaviors, using a daily diary format, is a common method of behavioral assessment for OCD and one that we routinely use in our clinic.

The information obtained from daily self-monitoring will only be as useful as the information requested on the form. Rather than just having the patient record on a blank sheet of paper, the clinican should devise forms to be used by the patient. The clinician might have a standard form that can be used by all patients or prefer to construct an individual recording sheet for each patient. In either case, at the very least, the therapist should require the recording of the frequency and severity of obsessive thoughts and ritualistic behaviors. The clinician also might find it useful to request that the patient make daily ratings of the degree of emotional distress. Additional types of information, including precipitating events and mood states, also may be recorded.

Like self-report inventories, self-monitoring can serve several functions. The most obvious is that of carefully monitoring behaviors on a daily basis. Through this daily assessment, behaviors not heretofore recognized as ritualistic might come to be identified. A common statement made by our obsessive–compulsive patients is that they do not know what is "normal" anymore. Daily self-monitoring provides a simple and direct method by which to detail the patient's symptomatology. It also provides information by which to assess treatment outcome. One potential difficulty in the use of self-monitoring procedures is patient compliance. Monitoring is a novel procedure for most patients. Therefore, initially it might be difficult to institute the procedures and secure compliance. Adherence also can be affected by the importance that the therapist places on the procedure. Clinicians who stress its necessity, and who take the time to review the forms in session, demonstrate the importance of self-monitoring and possibly increase compliance. We instruct our patients to make the ratings once per day, typically at bedtime. Although this probably sacrifices some accuracy, it increases compliance. Moreover, absolute accuracy is not necessarily the goal in using these procedures.

In some cases, self-monitoring behavior has been reported to decrease the frequency of the targeted behavior. *Reactivity* is theorized to occur because the act of recording the behavior cues the negative environmental consequences associated with the event. Therefore, recording serves as a reminder of the consequences, and the likelihood of performing the target behavior in the future is decreased. Such reactivity effects, to our knowledge, have not been reported for obsessive–compulsive behaviors. However, there are data indicating that, for certain categories of obsessive–compulsive patients (i.e., checkers), self-monitoring might actually function to increase the behavior (H. Rosenberg & Upper, 1983). The checking behavior of obsessive–compulsive patients appears to be predominantly aimed at the prevention of future events (Rachman, 1976). Inasmuch as checking centers on avoiding punishment, checkers might be reactive to the self-monitoring procedure in the same way as other anxiety disorders patients, that is by becoming more aware of the environmental consequences of the behavior. Only, in the case of checking patients, awareness of the consequences might serve to increase feelings of anxiety and fear of criticism and therefore function to increase the frequency of the rituals (which usually result in anxiety reduction). Clinicians should be aware of the possibility that self-monitoring might increase the frequency of rituals in patients with checking behaviors. Self-monitoring forms should be reviewed carefully with the patients to assess for the existence of this phenomenon.

In summary, self-monitoring is an effective procedure for assessing the daily behaviors of obsessive–compulsive patients. The form used to provide such information should be simple to use, quick to complete, and reviewed with the patients at each of their treatment sessions. Emphasizing the importance of completing the monitoring on a daily basis not only will provide important information on frequency and severity, but also might highlight important patterns such as changes in these variables due to day of the week or other environmental factors.

Psychophysiological Assessment

Patients with OCD often present at the initial assessment as highly anxious individuals. This anxiety might be described by these patients in terms of cognitive or somatic complaints. The clinician might also observe overt signs of anxiety including rapid speech, restlessness, and tremors. As noted by S. M. Turner and Michelson (1984), assessment of physiological variables might play an important role in understanding the etiology and maintenance of OCD, as well as in evaluating treatment response. Although there have been several studies that have assessed physiology as a result of treatment intervention (e.g., Boulougouris & Bassiakos, 1973), there has been little effort directed at assessing the natural role of physiology in OCD (S. M. Turner & Michelson, 1984).

Despite this limited attention, there have been several studies that have addressed the physiological responses of obsessive–compulsive patients in standardized assessment paradigms. In one of the earliest assessment studies, pulse rate variability was assessed in patients with compulsive handwashing behaviors prior to their touching a "contaminated" object, after touching the object, and after handwashing (Hodgson & Rachman, 1972). It was hypothesized that the patients would show increased pulse rate variability when in contact with the contaminated object and decreased variability after washing. Although the results did not reach the conventional .05 level of significance, there was a trend for the data to be in the hypothesized direction. This study, although providing some of the first data on physiological responses in obsessive–compulsive patients, suffers from several methodological weaknesses including small sample size, lack of a comparison or control group, and restriction to just one physiological measure.

Some of these weaknesses were addressed in a later study by Hornsveld, Kraaimaat, and Dam-Baggen (1979). Heart rate, skin conductance level and skin conductance spontaneous fluctuations were assessed in 6 patients with compulsive handwashing rituals and 12 psychiatric controls (diagnoses were unknown). Heart rate was assessed during a "neutral" handwashing phase, a relaxation phase, anticipation of touching a contaminated object, touching of a contaminated object, and handwashing after touching a contaminated object. Skin conductance level and spontaneous fluctuations were assessed only during the relaxation, anticipation, and touching phases. The results indicated that the compulsive patients had a higher number of spontaneous fluctuations when anticipating touching the contaminated object and when actually touching than the psychiatric control group. There were no differences between the groups on any of the measurement of heart rate or skin conductance level.

Some of the study's findings appeared quite paradoxical in that heart rate, when touching the contaminated object was 10 beats per minute lower than during either of the two handwashing periods. Thus, although these data provide some support for the notion that there are increased physiological responses in compulsive patients when in contact with a "fearful" stimulus, compared with a psychiatric control group, the data are ambiguous. Hornsveld et al. (1979) stressed the need to assess multiple channels of physiological responses, but it is disconcerting that in two studies (Hodgson & Rachman, 1972; Hornsveld et al., 1979) significant differences do not emerge on heart rate, considered the most potent response channel for OCD (Rachman & Hodgson, 1980).

Somewhat different results have been obtained when patients with severe obsessional ruminations but few or no compulsive behaviors were the object of clinical investigation (Rabavilas & Boulougouris, 1974). Heart rate, skin conductance, and spontaneous fluctuations were assessed in a group of 8 obsessional patients when comparing imagining obsessive imaginary and neutral imagery, flooding talk and neutral talk, and neutral talk condition and flooding in practice. When compared with neutral imagery, obsessional imagery resulted in a significant increase in heart rate and maximal deflection of skin conductance. Heart rate during flooding talk was also higher than heart rate during neutral talk. Flooding in practice also resulted in significantly higher heart rates, spontaneous fluctuations, and maximum deflection rate than the neutral-talk condition. This study, based on a within-sample comparison, indicates that increased physiological responses can be discerned in a carefully diagnosed sample of obsessional patients. However, to date no assessment study has addressed the issue of whether similar increases can be assessed in either a nonpatient group or a carefully diagnosed, psychiatric control sample. Until such between-group studies are completed, the role of physiological responses in the etiology and maintenance of OCD remains unclear.

For the practicing clinician, physiological assessment when the patient is in contact with the feared objects or situations can provide important corroborative data for the initial assessment. To conduct such a clinical physiological assessment, sophisticated equipment such as a polygraph is not required, although it obviously can be very useful. Assessment could include sophisticated measurements such as skin conductance, blood pressure and an electrocardiogram, or simple measurements such as counting pulse rate and respiration. Also, when planning either imaginal or in vivo flooding sessions, the clinician might wish to test the stimuli in a brief assessment session prior to beginning the treatment program. This assessment would allow the clinician the opportunity to be sure that the most relevant stimuli have been included in the designed intervention. Continued assessment of these physiological variables during treatment can also provide process data on the effectiveness of the chosen therapeutic intervention.

The four assessment procedures discussed thus far (interviewing, self-report inventories, self-monitoring, and psychophysiological assessments) represent the core strategies in the assessment armamentarium for obsessive–compulsive disorder. Clinicians working with obsessive–compulsive patients are advised to incorporate as many of these strategies into their standard practices as possible. Inclusion of data from more than one modality can provide a comprehensive clinical picture, as well as corroborative data on symptom improvement.

SECONDARY ASSESSMENT STRATEGIES

Other strategies have been employed in OCD. In addition to the four already discussed, procedures such as the Dexamethasone Suppression Test, sleep studies, and neurophysiological and neuropsychological testing also have been conducted with obsessive–compulsive patients. These procedures are not commonly used because they are often invasive, require elaborate equipment and specialized expertise, and, at the current time, do not appear to be critical for assessment or beneficial in the assessment of treatment outcome. At times, however, they can provide important information to clarify particular aspects of the clinical syndrome. The use of these procedures as they relate to the assessment of OCD will be described next.

Biological and Physical Assessments

In the early 1980s, the Dexamethasone Suppression Test (DST) received considerable attention as a potential diagnostic tool for depressive illnesses (e.g., Carroll et al., 1981). The DST consists of oral administration of dexamethasone (1 mg at 11 p.m.), followed by measurement of plasma cortisol levels the next day (at 8 a.m. and 4 p.m.). In individuals without psychiatric disorders, plasma cortisol remains suppressed for 24 hours following dexamethasone administration. However, approximately 40% to 60% of depressed patients fail to show this pattern of suppression, leading several researchers to postulate the existence of a neuroendocrine dysfunction in affective disorders.

The DST has been applied to patients with OCD (Asberg, Thoren, & Bertilsson, 1982; Cottraux, Bouvard, Claustrat, & Juenet, 1984; Insel, Kalin, Guttmacher, Cohen, & Murphy, 1982; Lieberman et al., 1985). In three of these studies (Asberg et al., 1982; Cottraux et al., 1984; Insel et al., 1982), 30% to 40% of the obsessive–compulsive patients failed to show the suppression pattern. This percentage is similar to the percentage reported for depressed patients. In the fourth study (Lieberman et al., 1985), there were no nonsuppressors among the obsessive–compulsive patients. This study differed from the other three in assessing plasma cortisol levels only at 4 p.m. rather that at 8 a.m. or 8 a.m. and 4 p.m. Those authors who have reported a significant percentage of nonsuppressors have suggested that obsessive–compulsive disorder and depression, although having different clinical pictures, might share a common biological substrate. More recently however, abnormal DSTs have been noted among many different patient groups, casting some doubt on this hypothesis. One explanation that is more parsimonious is that abnormal DSTs represent a general stress response, perhaps occurring in the most severe cases in any diagnostic category. A recent study by Mullen, Linsell, & Parker (1986) suggested that the findings obtained on DST tests can result from caloric restriction. Therefore, at this time it is not clear whether the DST has any relevance for OCD, and its utility with other disorders is also now in question.

Sleep studies, again similar to those that have often been conducted with affectively disordered patients, have been used in the assessment of obsessive–compulsive patients. Insel et al. (1982) reported that compared with normals, the sleep pattern of obsessive–compulsive patients was characterized by shallowness, frequent interruption, and insufficiency. In particular, similar to depressives, patients with OCD had a reduction in rapid eye movement efficiency and stage 4 sleep. The authors made several additional observations that present difficulty for the interpretation of these findings. First, fully one-half of the obsessive–compulsive patients also met criteria for depression, again perhaps indicating a shared biological substrate. However, some of the obsessive–compulsive patients had contamination fears and were quite upset at the possibility of being contaminated by the sleep-recording procedures. Therefore, it is possible that the sleep pattern of obsessive–compulsive patients in this study might have been a reaction to the sleep monitoring procedure (S. M. Turner, Beidel, et al., 1985).

In summary, these studies suggest that certain biological and physical characteristics of patients with OCD bear a strong resemblance to those of patients with affective disorders. This is not surprising in that a large number of obsessive–compulsive patients often present with a significant degree of depression. The presence of these biological and physical abnormalities does not imply that these two disorders are the same or that these assessments should be used to diagnose either obsessive–compulsive disorder or depression. At this stage, it is unclear if these anomalies exist in the individuals prior to the onset of these disorders. Without such information, the most parsimonious explanation remains that these characteristics might reflect, rather than diagnose or predict, the presence of extreme emotional upset in individuals with various types of disorders.

Neurophysiological and Neuropsychological Assessments

One of the main characteristics of OCD is the complaint of intrusive, involuntary thoughts or images. This complaint had led a number of investigators to study the brain activity of obsessive–compulsive patients in an attempt to find an explanation for these obsessional thoughts. In two studies examining average evoked potentials (Beech, Ciesielski, & Gordon, 1983; Ciesielski, Beech & Gordon, 1981), it was reported that, compared with normals, patients with obsessive–compulsive disorder had faster latencies and smaller amplitudes during visual attentional tasks. These studies have been criticized in that information-processing abnormalities (when compared with a control group) have been demonstrated in many psychiatric groups (cf., Spring & Zubin, 1978). More recently, Shagrass and his colleagues (Shagrass, Roemer, Straumanis, & Josiassen, 1984a, 1984b) used a finer grained analysis to delineate a more specific pattern of evoked potential variability that appeared to differentiate obsessive–compulsive patients from other diagnostic groups. The pattern appeared to involve the somatosensory-evoked potentials. The reader is referred to the Shagrass et al. (1984a, 1984b) studies for details. The authors acknowledged that the findings are difficult to interpret. In general, they suggested that brain function is deviant in some manner, but the specific mechanism(s) are not yet evident. Thus, like the biological and physical abnormalities, the meaning of these deviant findings is still unclear.

EEG functioning in patients with OCD has also been investigated. Although several studies have found few or no differences in the EEG recordings of these patients when compared with controls (Flor-Henry, Yeudall, Koles, & Howarth, 1979; Insel, Donnelly, Lalakea, Alterman, & Murphy, 1983), others have reported significant abnormalities, particularly in the temporal regions (Crighel & Solomonovici, 1968; Epstein & Bailine, 1971; Jenike & Brotman, 1984). The abnormalities suggest the possible presence of a hyperaroused state, but again, specific mechanisms have not been delineated. For a more detailed discussion of the role of neurophysiological and neuropsychological factors in OCD, see S. M. Turner, Beidel, and Nathan (1985).

Assessment of biological, physical, neurophysiological, and neuropsychological features might ultimately contribute to increased understanding of the disorder. In general, however, these procedures are used rather infrequently when assessing obsessive–compulsive patients. Although the results of these studies suggest that certain anomalies might exist, the relevance of these variables to the etiology of obsessive–compulsive disorder is still a matter of speculation and must be subjected to further empirical study. In addition, the importance of these variables in the treatment of OCD has yet to be demonstrated. These assessments should be used only when there is an indication that a significant abnormality of a particular type might exist.

SUMMARY AND CONCLUSIONS

The proper assessment of any disorder is critical for successful treatment. For the obsessional patient, proper and complete assessment is even more critical, due to the characteristics of the disorder and the secretive nature of the patient. The assessment process serves to document the range and intensity of the disorder, but also, in many instances, crucial aspects of the disorder are only elicited through careful use of the assessment strategy. In many instances, there is no substitute for observation in the natural environment (e.g., the home). Assessment should always include a thorough interview, which could require more than one session. Self-monitoring should always be a part of assessment and should be instituted immediately. Self-report inventories are also quite useful in helping develop a comprehensive picture of the patient's clinical status. Similarly, the use of psychophysiological measures can facilitate the assessment process, and they are frequently extremely useful in treatment. When there is evidence suggestive of an organic abnormality, the clinician might find neuropsychological or other biological tests helpful. Comprehensive assessment is the basis of the development and institution of an appropriate treatment program.

Chapter 4
Behavioral Treatment Strategies

PATIENT MANAGEMENT ISSUES

We have already discussed a number of management issues associated with obsessive–compulsive disorder. Here we want to point out a number of specific issues related to treatment. Obsessive patients are notoriously ambivalent about whether or not they should enter treatment. This issue is handled differently depending on individual patient characteristics. However, we usually describe the treatment in general terms and allow the patients to make the decision. We do not pressure patients to accept treatment because compliance requires considerable motivation. Once the treatment has been described, we are reluctant to repeat it in person or over the telephone, because we have found that such repetition does not aid the patients' attempts to make decisions. In many cases, the tendency to require multiple explanations is a manifestation of the disorder. However, it should always be a clinical decision as to how much explanation is required. We do not describe the treatment in detail until we are ready to start the program because patients rarely understand it fully prior to that time, and such a description can in itself create considerable anticipatory anxiety.

Obsessional patients often attempt to negotiate how the treatment is to be conducted. Usually this involves what the flooding sessions will include or to which rituals response prevention will be directed. Although patients sometimes have a good reason for such suggestions, more often than not this is a manifestation of avoidance. Also, such behavior is sometimes associated with the personality attributes of obsessive–compulsive personality or other personality features (e.g., control). When this occurs, patients are informed, as noted before, that the nature of the treatment for this disorder requires that it be implemented in a certain way and that failure to do so usually results in ineffective treatment. Thus, the therapist must have the leeway to decide how the treatment is to be implemented. This is usually sufficient for all but the most disturbed (particularly from a personality standpoint) patients.

Many obsessive patients, particularly those who have had the disorder for a long time, do not believe the treatment will be effective because they have tried so many other approaches. In these cases, we offer encouragement by conveying our belief in our approach to treatment and providing some information regarding outcome studies. However, we are careful in all cases to apprise patients that we cannot guarantee a positive outcome. Similarly, we are careful in describing how much improvement can be expected. Typically, we indicate that about 70% of patients treated in this fashion improve, but we point out that how much a patient improves depends on a number of variables such as ability to adhere to the treatment regimen, complications such as medical and other psychiatric conditions, chronicity of the disorder, and interpersonal and other psychosocial stressors that might be associated with their condition. In describing the improvement in patients treated in our clinic, our usual response is that about 95% of those patients who adhere to the treatment regimen and remain in treatment for a satisfactory period of time show some improvement. The degree of improvement varies considerably and is often related to a host of other parameters.

An important part of our preparation of patients for treatment is to inform them that their disorder is a chronic condition and that they will have to learn to understand themselves and their limitations in order to manage and control it. Further, they are told that they will likely continue to have some vestiges of the disorder following treatment and might very well experience worsening of the symptoms during periods of stress. The intent is to prepare patients for the fact that they are not likely to be totally asymptomatic following the treatment program and to prepare them for the maintenance phase of treatment, during which efforts will be made to help them learn methods of self-management. Moreover, we often use the analogy of diabetes and hypertension to prepare them for the necessity of taking an active role in helping to control their disorder by managing the stressors in their lives. We believe this is a realistic approach that prepares patients for the fact that they are unlikely to be totally symptom free and for the need to assume some responsibility for themselves.

In this chapter, we will discuss the primary, as well as some of the more secondary, behavioral treatments used in treating obsessive–compulsive disorder. Since the seminal work of Victor Meyer (Meyer, 1966), behavioral treatment strategies have emerged as the major intervention for this disorder. Indeed, Foa, Steketee, and Ozarow (1985) concluded from their review of the literature that response prevention and flooding (exposure) are now the treatments of choice for obsessions and compulsions. Of the behavioral treatments, we concur in this assessment, and certainly there is no literature demonstrating any other treatment to reach the approximately 70% effectiveness rate achieved by response prevention and flooding. However, as described, there are other behavioral and nonbehavioral interventions that might have a role in the treatment of this disorder, particularly in various subtypes. In addition, in chapter 7 we will discuss the role of follow-up treatment in maintenance and the use of various strategies to maintain treatment gains. For the past 8 years, we have employed a standard treatment strategy (inpatient and outpatient) for most obsessive–compulsive patients in our Anxiety Disorders Clinic. We will begin our discussion of behavioral treatments by describing these strategies. The reader should keep in mind that although this approach has proved effective for most patients, alterations are necessary in many instances. Thus, the strategy is viewed as flexible and requires the exercise of considerable clinical judgment for effective implementation.

FLOODING AND RESPONSE PREVENTION

The central elements in the program employed in our clinic consist of flooding and response prevention, as we have noted. There are two basic strategies, one for inpatient treatment and one for outpatient treatment. In the case of outpatient treatment, which is used for about 80% of the patients we see, a program consisting of 10 consecutive days of flooding and response prevention is implemented. Patients are required to come to the clinic on a daily basis where imaginal or in vivo flooding, or both, are conducted. Sessions last for a minimum of $1\frac{1}{2}$ hours but are typically continued until within-session habituation is achieved. To determine when habituation has been achieved, we use both subjective and objective indexes (e.g., heart rate and Subjective Units of Distress ratings). However, clinical judgment also is needed here. The problem of dysynchrony is well known. Thus, it would not be unusual for a patient to report no distress during a flooding session, although exhibiting high heart rate, or vice versa. In such cases, the therapist must use his or her clinical judgment to decide how to proceed.

In addition to the flooding sessions within the clinic, a home-based response prevention and flooding program is implemented. As discussed, the aid of a significant other might be used to accomplish this goal. Although we favor complete response prevention, in some instances a graded approach is used. The use of a therapist-assisted, home-based flooding or response prevention program, or both, might be necessary for a number of reasons, including (a) the patient is unable to discontinue the ritual, (b) significant others are unavailable or unsuitable, (c) the patient is unable or refuses exposure to feared stimuli, and (d) the existence of other rituals or avoidance behavior is suspected or the therapist believes a home visit is necessary to fully understand the symptom picture. Thus, in some instances, we decide on a home visit even if the patient feels the program is working well.

We mentioned the issue of graded versus complete flooding and response prevention earlier. The program we employ can be adapted to either approach, although we have indicated already our preference for the complete strategy. We might select a gradual approach if we feel there are simply too many behaviors to handle otherwise. For example, a patient with pervasive contamination fears and pervasive cognitive rituals might be best handled by separating the disorder into those two components and treating them sequentially. Similarly, for clinical reasons, we sometimes decide to grade the intensity of the exposure, particularly in those few patients who are able to do the flooding and response prevention without supervision. Figures 4.1 through 4.5 illustrate the response of 5 patients over a 10-day treatment regimen of response prevention and flooding. These patients had been involved in an experimental study of the drug fluoxetine before being treated behaviorally (see S. M. Turner, Beidel, Stanley, & Jacob, in press). They were not on any drugs during the behavioral treatment. As can be seen, four of the patients showed a good response. However, little change was achieved in one of the patients.

When the decision is made to hospitalize an obsessive–compulsive patient, the patient is informed to expect a minimum 3-week hospital stay. The majority of our patients are not kept longer than the 3 weeks. Following behavioral assessment, a 24-hour response prevention program is initiated. Ward personnel are assigned to the patient on a continuous basis. In addition to the response prevention, periods of imaginal flooding, in vivo flooding, or both, are instituted. These sessions are conducted in an identical fashion as the outpatient sessions, except that more than one session might be held on any given day.

A few days before discharge, the extent of the supervision is gradually lessened in preparation for leaving the hospital. Anticipatory anxiety increases at this point but usually decreases if satisfactory reentry is achieved. Depending on the individual, we conduct a home visit on the first day of discharge to ensure that response prevention is continued in a satisfactory manner. Also, we have found this to be an important aspect of treatment in certain cases. The presence of the therapist in the home seems to be reassuring, and we can quickly get any trouble spots under control. The duration of the home visit varies from patient to patient, as

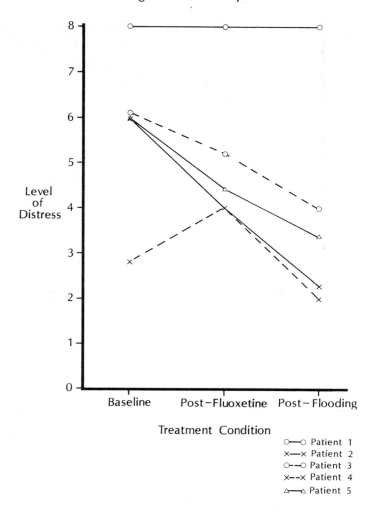

FIGURE 4.1. Daily Distress.

does the number of visits required. However, we rarely make more than three visits to the home (or any other relevant setting), and each visit is typically 1 day long. Patients are seen immediately in outpatient treatment following discharge. The frequency of outpatient visits is determined by individual patient characteristics but usually ranges from two to three visits per week, with descending frequency over the following few weeks. Figure 4.6 depicts the changes in a patient treated on one of our inpatient units. Full details can be found in S. M. Turner et al. (1979).

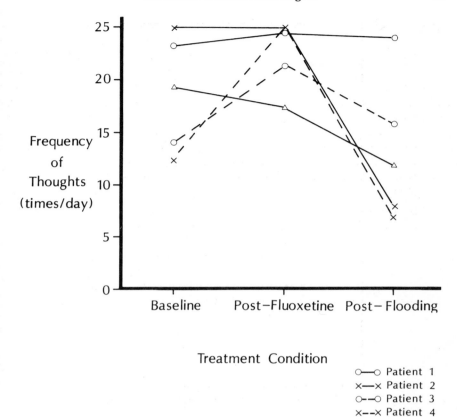

FIGURE 4.2. Frequency of Daily Obsessional Thoughts.

Considerations in Implementing Flooding and Response Prevention

There are a number of factors to be considered that could affect the implementation and effectiveness of any flooding and response prevention program. Those that have particular relevance for programs with obsessive–compulsive patients are listed next. This list represents a synthesis of our own experience and recommendations contained in Marks (1985).

1. *Evaluate the patient for depressive symptomatology, and, if necessary, treat the depression.* In treating such patients, we have found that habituation during flooding frequently is not achieved until depression is relieved.

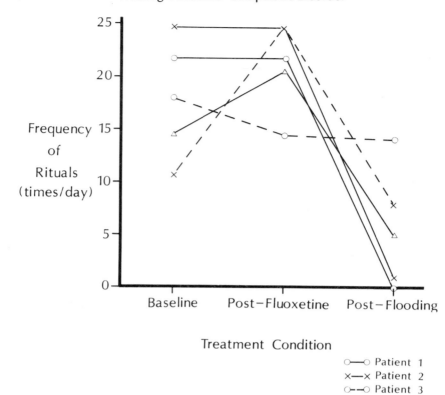

FIGURE 4.3. Frequency of Daily Rituals.

Foa (1979) has confirmed this in an experimental study. Also, relief from depression tends to correlate with increased motivation to confront feared stimuli, increased confidence that the patient can successfully do it, and improved attitude about the ultimate treatment outcome.

2. *Discontinue or reduce to minimum levels any alcohol or anxiolytic agents being used by the patient.* Inpatient hospitalization might be required for this if the patient is physiologically addicted or there are other reasons to suspect that outpatient withdrawal is unsafe. One reason for the discontinuation of these agents is that exposure treatments appear to be more effective if the anxiety is not blocked pharmacologically during the treatment. Also, chances for maintenance are improved when the use of alcohol or anxiolytics is not an issue.

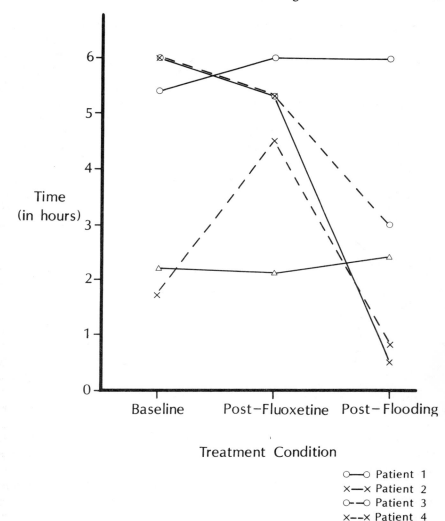

FIGURE 4.4. Time Spent in Obsessional Ideation.

3. *Evaluate the patient for the presence of medical disorders.* Such disorders as cardiovascular diseases, asthma, peptic ulcer, and ulcerative colitis can be aggravated by anxiety, and, if they are present, they could influence the manner in which flooding is implemented. For example, flooding might have to be conducted in a gradual fashion to control the level of anxiety. In our experience, gradual flooding is less effective with

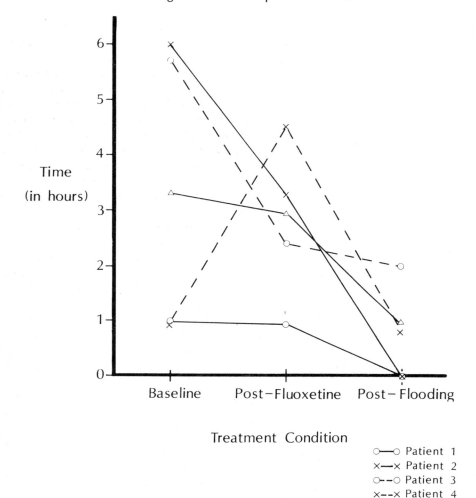

FIGURE 4.5. Time Spent Engaged in Rituals.

obsessive–compulsive patients. Therefore, treatment might have to be delayed until the patient's medical condition is such that treatment is reasonably safe. In some instances, it could be better to conduct the treatment in an inpatient setting.

4. *Define the problem in precise, behavioral terms.* Good examples include "I am afraid of contracting diseases by using public restrooms" or "I have to wash my hands more than 50 times per day." Complaints such as "I

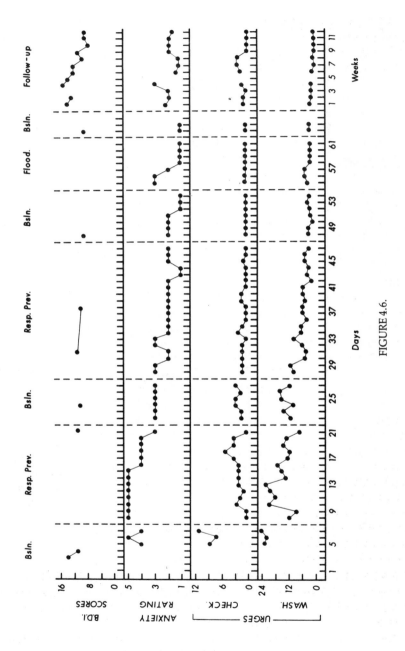

FIGURE 4.6.

57

am terribly anxious" do not lend themselves to flooding programs. When imaginal flooding is used, the therapist must take special care to include all of the relevant fear cues in the imaginal scene. Thus, if an individual avoids driving due to fear that she or he might injure a child, the scene must contain stimuli involving children along with the associated catastrophic consequences. The reader is referred to Lang and colleagues (Lang, Kozak, Miller, Levin, & McLean, 1980; Lang, Levin, Miller, & Kozak 1983) for a discussion of types of fear cues important for exposure treatments.

5. *Make sure that the patient is willing to invest the large blocks of time necessary for treatment to be successful.* Flooding and response prevention are time-consuming procedures and daily practice is necessary. Similarly, the therapist must be willing to invest the large amount of time that might be dictated by what happens in individual sessions. Although not all behavior therapists subscribe to the notion that within-session habituation must be achieved for flooding to be successful, we have found treatment to be more successful when conducted in this fashion. Foa (1979) provided some support for this approach when she demonstrated that for between-session habituation to occur, within-session habituation must have been achieved, although the achievement of within-session habituation does not guarantee between-session habituation. We have found the amount of time required for within-session habituation to vary widely among patients, ranging from less than an hour to as many as 6 hours.

6. *Ensure that relatives end their cooperation in carrying out rituals.* The behavior of relatives and friends can play an important role in the patient's care. In some instances, they are able to assist in conducting the flooding sessions or the response prevention program. If relatives or friends are to play a role in the treatment program, they need to attend the therapy sessions so that they can be given detailed instructions and so that their involvement can be monitored. One must be cautious in using family members or spouses in the treatment program because they frequently fail to understand the disorder, even after careful explanation, and frequently the relationships are already strained. Participation in the treatment program can further aggravate relationships that are already tenuous.

7. *Enlist the assistance of a cotherapist when necessary to assure adequate duration of the flooding sessions and to aid in home visits or in vivo flooding.* It is incumbent upon the primary therapist to assure that the therapeutic procedures are being carried out consistently by all other therapists and significant others assisting in the treatment. In our experience, this requires close and constant supervision.

Variations in Conducting Flooding and Response Prevention

Although flooding and response prevention remain the behavioral treatments of choice for patients with obsessive–compulsive disorder, many variations have been empirically investigated. These include the form of stimulus presentation, the duration of exposure, and the importance of the therapist's presence during the actual exposure session. The most important considerations are discussed later. For a comprehensive review of this literature, the reader is referred to Foa et al. (1985).

Once a therapist has decided to use a flooding and response prevention paradigm, one of the first decisions to be made concerns the manner in which the fearful stimuli will be presented (imaginally, in vivo, or both). Early studies comparing the singular use of each modality did not find any differences between imaginal and in vivo exposure. As noted by Foa, Steketee, & Ozarow (1985), these studies did not include a great deal of attention to the content of the stimuli or its relevance to patient symptomatology. Although it is generally accepted that in vivo exposure is superior and preferable, there do appear to be certain instances when imaginal exposure proves more effective. For example, when anxiety is fueled by the possible disastrous consequences of an event (e.g., death, destruction), imaginal flooding may be the modality of choice, due to its ability to include graphic descriptions of these feared events (Foa, Steketee, Turner, & Fischer, 1980). In a small number of cases, we have found imaginal exposure effective when in vivo exposure had proved ineffective or less than satisfactory. We suspect that in such instances, one factor might be whether or not the patient engages in forms of cognitive avoidance during in vivo exposure. Presentation of the imaginal scene in a continuous fashion could prevent such avoidance. Furthermore, verbal elaboration contained in imaginal scenes might serve to enhance the fear cues. In addition, it appears that a combination of imaginal and in vivo exposure might be most effective in maintaining treatment gains for those whose symptom picture includes thoughts of disastrous consequences (Foa et al. 1980) or for those with more complex and less coherent fear structures, that is, obsessive–compulsive disorder versus simple phobia (Foa, Steketee, & Grayson, 1985).

Several studies have reported that audiotapes and videotapes have proven useful in assisting the patient in imagining the fearful events, thus aiding the flooding process. Salkovskis (1983) reported the successful treatment of ruminations centering on violent thoughts toward others using such a strategy. The thoughts were audiotaped and the patient listened to the tape for 90 minutes at a time. Over a period of 4 months, the daily frequency of the ruminations decreased from an average of 30 times a day to zero. Similarly, Thyer (1985) reported using an audiotaped description of a patient's obsession over harming her daughter with a knife to successfully extinguishing these intrusive thoughts. We have employed such a strategy with a minority of patients treated in our clinic and have found it to be useful in some cases.

A number of clinical issues will determine whether or not this is a viable strategy, including confidence in the patient's ability to follow instructions, the patient's mood state, and confidence in the patient's ability to provide accurate reports. The effectiveness of imaginal-exposure procedures hinges upon the patient's ability to vividly reproduce the anxiety-producing situation. Without this ability, the intervention is ineffective. At times, we have used sound-effects records to enhance the subject's ability to imagine a particular situation. Videotaped exposure sessions also have been used in the inpatient treatment of a woman with fears of contamination of her home by food particles (Beidel, Turner, & Allgood-Hill, 1986). Her disorder was so severe that she had to be hospitalized. After she claimed that she was unable to imagine the feared home situations, videotapes of her home contaminated by the feared substances were shown to her in daily flooding sessions. Twelve daily flooding sessions decreased the daily frequency of her obsessional thinking by 50%. Although videotape was not as effective as in vivo exposure, these examples illustrate the successful use of audiotape or videotape to augment a flooding program. The applications are limited only by the therapist's creativity.

The therapist also is faced with other treatment decisions including the duration of exposure sessions, the frequency of exposure sessions (massed or spaced), and the use of gradual or rapid exposure. Concerning the duration of exposure, there is some evidence that long-exposure sessions are more beneficial than briefer sessions. This is particularly so when the stimuli are presented in vivo. The most crucial variable affecting treatment appears to be the total amount of exposure time (Foa, Steketee, & Ozarow, 1985). However, in our experience, massed exposure sessions are usually more beneficial than spaced practice.

A related decision is whether the exposure should be conducted in gradual or rapid fashion. With gradual exposure, the fearful elements are graded along a hierarchy, and stimuli are presented in order from the least to the most fearful, whereas in rapid exposure, the individual is immediately exposed to all of or the most fear-producing stimuli. There does not appear to be any clear-cut evidence from the experimental literature to support the use of one method over the other. Hodgson, Rachman, and Marks (1972) reported both procedures to be equally effective in reducing OCD symptoms, although patients felt more comfortable when fearful stimuli were presented gradually. We have noted that in the case of obsessive–compulsive patients, rapid exposure appears to deliver the best results. In fact, in a number of cases where both procedures were used, patients have commented that they feel the rapid treatment is more useful. In obsessional patients, it must be remembered that the anxiety-producing obsessions are persistent, unlike in focal phobias. Thus, the patient has much time between sessions to think about the fears.

The issue of patient comfort during the flooding session highlights an error commonly committed by novice therapists, who often encourage the patient to use relaxation skills while being exposed to feared stimuli. This is counterproductive to the goals of the flooding paradigm, and it cannot be supported on either theoretical or empirical grounds. Flooding treatment is based on an extinction and habituation model that postulates that prolonged direct contact with the fearful stimulus is necessary if anxiety is to diminish. Relaxation exercises function to direct the patient's attention away from the stimulus and could serve as a barrier between the patient and complete contact. In fact, the relaxation would function much like alcohol or anxiolytic drugs in blocking the experience of anxiety.

The relative merit of attention or distraction during the flooding session was empirically investigated in two studies by Grayson, Foa, and Steketee (1982, 1986). In the preliminary study, using a cross-sectional design (Grayson et al., 1982), patients were exposed to their most feared contaminant under attention-focusing or distracting conditions. Attention focusing consisted of direct contact with the stimulus and conversing with a therapist about the feared contaminant. In the distraction condition, the patient was in direct contact with the stimulus but played a videogame with the therapist. Each subject was treated with a 90-minute exposure session under each condition, on each of 2 consecutive days. When attention focusing preceded distraction, greater between-session habituation and greater synchrony (covariation) between heart rate and subjective anxiety was noted, suggesting that exposure is more effective when attention remains stimulus focused (Grayson et al., 1982).

In an extension of the earlier study, Grayson et al. (1986) used a between-subject design in which OCD patients had two 90-minute flooding sessions with either the attention-focusing or the distraction variation. Sessions occurred on subsequent days. Attention focusing produced significantly larger within-session heart rate habituation than did distraction, but there were no between-group differences in subjective anxiety. However, in contrast with the earlier study, there was no between-session habituation for either group. The authors postulated several possible explanations for the lack of habituation in the second study, and the interested reader is referred to the publication for this discussion.

Despite this discrepancy, the weight of the theoretical and empirical evidence appears to argue against distraction, and attention-focusing instructions are recommended as the most conservative treatment strategy. That is certainly consistent with our clinical experience. As we have noted, it is when the patient avoids or otherwise is allowed to escape focusing on the feared stimuli that problems in treatment occur.

As noted in chapter 3, therapeutic style can also have a substantial impact upon treatment success. A related question is whether the therapist's presence during the actual exposure session is necessary for successful outcome. Based on the results of two studies, therapist presence would appear to be unnecessary (Emmelkamp & de Lange, 1983; Emmelkamp & Kraanen, 1977). In the first study (Emmelkamp & Kraanen, 1977), self-controlled exposure was as effective as therapist-controlled exposure in reducing OCD symptoms. In the second study (Emmelkamp & de Lange, 1983), self-controlled exposure was compared with partner-controlled exposure. Although both groups were significantly improved at posttreatment, the partner-assisted group improved more. However, the self-controlled group continued to improve such that at 1 month follow-up there were no significant treatment effects between conditions.

Although these studies suggest that therapist assistance is not vital, we believe that therapist involvement is crucial in most instances. The decision to employ self-controlled exposure should be made on a clinical basis rather than on a diagnostic one. We believe this is particularly important for the first few flooding sessions. Our reasoning is based upon our experience with the many ways OCD patients can "flood themselves" and still avoid fearful stimuli at the same time. We have seen patients claim they are touching a "contaminant"; but they were using one fingertip instead of the entire hand. Patients often claim they have forgotten how to "act normal" and accompanying them on the first few sessions ensures that they are carrying out the instructions in the necessary manner. Once the therapist is assured of this, further sessions can be conducted on a self-exposed basis following the therapist's instructions. Another reason for accompanying patients on the first few flooding sessions is that it provides an excellent opportunity for detailed observation of their actual behavior when in contact with the stimulus. This often reveals other rituals that have not been divulged because of embarrassment or fear or simply because the patients had not recognized them as rituals. Physiological, cognitive, and overt-motoric behaviors can be assessed. We have found the first flooding session invaluable in terms of increasing understanding of patients' symptomatology and uncovering previously unreported rituals, obsessions, and fears. If self-directed exposure is to be used, we recommend that the therapist conduct at least the first few sessions.

Response Prevention

We have primarily discussed flooding up to this point. Now we would like to turn to response prevention, the other intervention we consider to be part of the primary treatment components necessary in the treatment of obsessive–compulsive patients. As we noted in our discussion of flooding, we consider response prevention to be in large part another method of ensuring exposure to the feared stimuli. However, there are some additional characteristics of response prevention that might be essential for successful treatment. Response prevention ensures that the patient does not engage in ritualistic activities that in most cases result in anxiety reduction. In those cases that result in anxiety elevation, one reason for this appears to be the patient's negative self-evaluation following the rituals (e.g., "this is another example of my failure or inability to control"). In this instance, prevention of the ritual prevents the elevation of anxiety cued by negative evaluation. Thus, prevention of the ritualistic response serves a therapeutic function regardless of whether rituals are anxiety reducing, anxiety elevating, or both.

Typically, however, response prevention is seen as a strategy to prevent reinforcement of the repetitive behavior through anxiety reduction. In general, the patient should be prevented from carrying out any ritualistic behavior. However, some caveats are in order. *First*, it is our policy not to ask the patient to do anything that we would not do ourselves. For example, handling garbage or refuse and then not being allowed to wash the hands before eating is unacceptable in our opinion. Another example might be that of not allowing a patient to take a daily shower, when denying such an activity violates American cultural norms. With a little creativity, these situations can be avoided. To illustrate this point, in the latter example, the patient could be allowed a brief shower and then be subjected immediately to "recontamination." We believe this is preferable to practices that might entail hygienic risk, might alienate the patient, and might be viewed by the public as cruel. *Second*, as a rule, we do not physically prevent a patient from engaging in rituals. The patient must agree to abide by the treatment plan, and he or she is fully informed that we will help through distraction, redirection, or cajoling. However, it is made clear that continuation of treatment is contingent on the patients' adherence to the treatment plan. Therapists need to have a repertoire of discussion topics, activities, or both available to assist in the distraction process. With an individual who engages in counting or other cognitive rituals, it is often difficult to determine performance of the ritual because it is internal. Thus, more motivation is required on the part of the patient because the therapist must rely upon the patient to inform her or him of the urge. *Third,* the therapist must be attuned to the likelihood that the patient will engage in behaviors not reported to be rituals because he or she does not view them as rituals, is unaware of them, or purposefully conceals them. For example, one patient with massive contamination fears and cleaning rituals would keep her refrigerator shelves covered with paper towels. She did not inform us of this behavior because she did not view it as a compulsive ritual. Yet, it was clearly a behavior designed to prevent contamination and was carried out in ritualistic fashion. Failure to eliminate these types of behavior could affect outcome and maintenance. *Finally,* patients could engage in any number of behaviors that appear to be anxiety reducing while they are technically adhering to instructions. For example, they might verbally check with others or get others to actually perform a particular act that will alleviate their anxiety. Behaviors that involve acts such as visual checking or cognitive rituals are particularly susceptible to this problem.

OTHER BEHAVIORAL INTERVENTIONS

In addition to exposure, there are other therapeutic interventions that have been used as components of a successful behavioral treatment regimen with OCD patients. For example, Foa, Steketee, and Ozarow (1985) described a number of these interventions as *blocking procedures.* This term was used because these treatments are designed to prevent engagement in the ritual that results in anxiety decrement. The most frequently used blocking procedure is response prevention, which has been discussed, although our own conceptualization of response prevention is consistent with its being a special case of flooding (cf. Baum, 1970), which seems to be different from Foa and colleagues' viewpoint. Thus, in our standard approach, response prevention is used to attain extinction of the anxiety response by preventing the anxiety-reducing ritual (thereby forcing the patient to be continually exposed to the feared stimuli).

Another procedure sometimes used to block obsessions or cognitive rituals is thought-stopping. This procedure pairs the evocation of the obsessional thought with the shouting of the word "stop." After repeated pairings, the shouting is faded to a normal voice tone, then to a whisper, and finally the patient need only think the word "stop" to successfully dispel the thought. Patients are given regular homework assignments to practice the strategy on a daily basis at a frequency appropriate for individual cases. An example of the implementation of thought-stopping can be found in S. M. Turner, Holzman, and Jacob (1983). In reviewing the literature on thought-stopping, Foa, Steketee, and Ozarow (1985) noted that, although the early case reports of the effectiveness of thought-stopping were quite promising, later controlled studies did not support this initial optimism (Emmelkamp & Kwee, 1977; Stern, 1978; Stern, Lipsedge, & Marks, 1975). We view thought-stopping as a weak intervention at best and typically use it during the maintenance phase of treatment when the patient's emotional distress has improved considerably and when obsessions are most likely to be less intense. Even under these circumstances, our experience is that thought-stopping is of limited value for most obsessional patients. Thus, we are forced to conclude that, although thought-stopping might be effective in isolated cases, it cannot be recommended as a primary treatment modality for obsessive–compulsive disorder.

With the advent of cognitive therapy (Beck, 1976), it was only a matter of time before cognitive approaches were applied to the treatment of obsessive–compulsive disorder. Robertson, Wendiggensen, and Kaplan (1983) presented three case reports in which cognitive restructuring, accompanied by a traditional exposure program, was effective in treating three OCD patients. Salkovskis (1985) has proposed a cognitive–behavioral analysis of OCD. In this conceptualization, the intrusive thought is viewed as the stimulus (in this case, cognitive stimulus) that precipitates the emotional responses. Adopting the three-systems model of fear (Lang, 1977), the cognitive *response* to the emotional distress is the belief in personal responsibility or guilt over the result of the anxiety-evoking event. For example, intrusive thoughts such as "touching money will result in the spread of disease" serve as the precipitating event for evoking anxiety, whereas the thought "If anyone in my family dies, it will be my fault because I touched dirty money" is the cognitive response, in the three-system model, to that anxiety-provoking event. Rituals can then be conceptualized as behavioral correction for the "bad thing" that has occurred and as an attempt to rid oneself of blame for disastrous consequences. It is not our intention to discuss the merits of this conceptual model here; for a comprehensive discussion of the model the reader is referred to Salkovskis (1985).

However, when conceptualized in this fashion, OCD symptomatology appears similar to that of phobic disorders, and the adaptation of cognitive therapy (Beck & Emery, 1985) to the treatment of obsessive–compulsive disorder would seem to be feasible. The therapist would focus on the intrusive thoughts in a somewhat different fashion with the emphasis on cognitive consequences, that is, the resultant feelings of blame or guilt. For those OCD patients for whom standard behavior therapy is not always effective (e.g., those with overvalued ideation), it seems reasonable to speculate that an intervention with greater emphasis on cognitive content might improve treatment success.

Salkovskis and Warwick (1985) recently reported the use of cognitive therapy to treat a patient with obsessive–compulsive disorder. This patient expressed the strong conviction that she would contract cancer if she did not clean and avoid any form of ultraviolet light. This woman appeared to meet the criteria for overvalued ideation as defined by Foa (1979). Typical exposure sessions did not result in within-session habituation. As we have already indicated, overvalued ideation is used to describe the thinking of obsessional patients who do not see entirely the irrationality of their thinking. For example, in our clinic we evaluated a woman with extensive cleaning rituals centered around fear of contamination with asbestos. Although her home had contained asbestos at one time, it had been removed. Nevertheless, this patient believed that the threat still remained and did not consider her behavior to be unjustified. At the time of our evaluation, she was significantly depressed and managed only a few hours of sleep at night, and her marital relationship was seriously impaired. Such patients are considered to have a poor treatment prognosis. Indeed, the patient described would not accept treatment if it involved altering her beliefs. Obviously, this behavior is reminiscent of a monosymptomatic delusion. We have discussed this issue in chapter 2 and will not repeat it here.

In the case reported by Sakovskis and Warwick, cognitive therapy was directed at the thoughts that resulted from the intrusive stimulus, "ultraviolet light causes cancer." The resultant thoughts took the form "I have used cosmetics exposed to ultraviolet light," "I will get a disfiguring skin cancer because I have used these contaminated cosmetics," and so on. Cognitive therapy was applied to the second set of thoughts, and several sessions of examining the evidence for and against these statements resulted in a weakening, but not a remission, of the thoughts. Exposure therapy was then reinstituted with resultant within- and between-session habituation and a reduction in rituals.

In discussing this case, the authors credited the cognitive therapy with changing the "automatic thoughts" following the anxiety-evoking stimulus and making the patient more receptive to the reinstitution of the flooding program. Following cognitive therapy, she responded to the flooding session more like a "typical obsessional" rather than in the style characteristic of patients with overvalued ideation. However, as also noted by the authors, the importance of the exposure session following the cognitive therapy cannot be overlooked. It is difficult to determine exactly what the critical variables were in this case. Yet, it is clear that flooding was necessary to achieve meaningful reduction in the symptoms.

At this point, it is unclear what role cognitive therapy might play in the treatment armamentarium for obsessive–compulsive disorder, and controlled experimental studies are needed. Interestingly, Beidel and Turner (1986) argued that there is really little difference between classic behavioral and more cognitively oriented treatment because both tend to involve extensive exposure. The reader is referred to that article for a more detailed discussion of the issues. Should future studies show that cognitive therapy is useful as an initial treatment for overvalued ideation, this would be extremely valuable because those patients with overvalued ideation are thought to be at least one subgroup that does not respond very well to current treatments. At the present, the best approach would appear to be to consider cognitive therapy as an adjunct to treatment, much like thought-stopping.

INPATIENT VERSUS OUTPATIENT TREATMENT

At some time, every therapist will be faced with the decision of whether to treat a patient as an inpatient or an outpatient. Many patients can be treated as outpatients, but each case must be evaluated on its own merit. Although inpatient hospitalization can be very disruptive, some patients can take temporary work leave or sick time to undergo hospitalization if necessary. Hospitalization would be necessary if (a) detoxification is needed; (b) the patient lives far from the treatment facility and is unable to travel for daily treatment sessions; (c) there is a question as to whether the response prevention can be successfully implemented in the patient's home (i.e., the patient is unable to follow instructions or the family members are unable to assist); (d) the patient is significantly depressed and suicide issues, medication issues, or both dictate admission; (e) the patient's medical status is such that a controlled environment is needed.

With respect to enlisting the assistance of a significant other, it is essential that the strength of the relationship be carefully evaluated. In many instances, the marital relationship has become so strained that asking a spouse to play this role is contraindicated. One strategy we have often used is to begin treatment as an inpatient until the most disruptive symptoms are reduced and the individual has regained a sense of control. Once the gross symptoms and the patient's level of distress have been reduced, outpatient treatment with the assistance of a significant other is more likely to be successful. The reduction of the symptoms and the clear evidence that change can be made is often a motivational factor for family members.

THE PROBLEM OF COGNITIVE RITUALS

Cognitive rituals present a particular challenge to the therapist and deserve special attention. Cognitive rituals are acts such as the recitation of a series of numbers "in the head" in a particular fashion or the need to think certain thoughts in a particular sequence. Cognitive rituals differ from obsessions and ruminations in that they have a particular pattern and have a specific termination point. Such behaviors can be very difficult to treat because they are internal. In some instances, patients can report urges to engage in the cognitive rituals and can be prevented from doing so. Other patients, however, are unable to do this, or the behaviors appear in response to contact with various stimuli and thus occur in rapid fashion without urges. In many instances, the successful treatment of cognitive rituals depends on the ability to "instigate" the rituals and then intervene to prevent them from being completed. Here, in particular, the creativity of the therapist is likely to be taxed. For example, we are currently treating a patient who mentally goes through his work in a set sequence for a specific number of times before being satisfied that it was done properly. The sequence is cued by attempts to leave work that is completed. He does not go back to check overtly. To institute response prevention in this case required the availability of the patient at the completion of his work. At that point, the patient was led to engage in a number of activities to prevent the cognitive ritual.

OBSESSIONAL SLOWNESS

A small subset of obsessive–compulsive patients present for treatment with what can be described as *obsessional slowness*. Behaviors such as brushing teeth, dressing, washing, and combing hair take an excessive amount of time. At times, these behaviors appear to be a deliberate effort at procrastination and clearly serve an active avoidance function. Sometimes, the components of these behaviors become ritualized (Jacob, Ford, & Turner, 1985). Attempts to speed up the activities create anxiety and doubt that the behavior was performed correctly; thus the patient resists directions to increase the speed of functioning. Although in our experience this condition usually occurs in conjunction with other OCD characteristics, there are reports of cases of primary obsessional slowness where this characteristic is present without evidence of ritualistic behaviors (Rachman, 1974; Rachman & Hodgson, 1980).

We have seen several patients who were referred to our clinic with primary obsessional slowness as the referral diagnosis. When evaluating a patient for primary obsessional slowness, clinicians should keep in mind that other conditions such as psychomotor retardation or intellectual deficiency might play a role in an individual's daily functioning. One patient was referred to us for treatment of primary obsessional slowness due to her inability to complete her activities of daily living in a timely fashion. For example, she would become "frozen" in the shower or on the staircase and had to be moved physically by another individual. When asked about her thoughts during those episodes, she replied that she was thinking about what she had to do that day, which resulted in marked distress. She was recently divorced and living on her own for the first time. An intelligence test revealed an IQ of 75, casting a new light on her overall symptom picture. Many of her symptoms were only partially due to obsessionality. Some of the behaviors were due to being overwhelmed by having to cope with independent living, a condition for which she was totally unprepared. She was placed in a halfway house and with this support and guidance the extreme slowness disappeared.

We have seen other cases of similar slowness that were not accompanied by low intelligence. In these cases, the treatment plan consisted of speeding up the patient's activities. The patient is given a time limit in which to complete each task (two minutes for brushing teeth, five minutes for showering, etc.). The time limits are enforced by the inpatient staff, a family member, or patient self-restraint. Tasks not completed within the time limit are left unfinished for that day. At first, these time limits create a great deal of anxiety for the patient (just as response prevention initially creates a great deal of anxiety for other obsessionals), and the therapist should be prepared to assist the patient in coping with this distress. Over the course of several days the patient's ability to complete the tasks within the time limits will improve, and the anxiety surrounding the time limits will lessen. All of the caveats regarding the implementation of response-prevention programs also apply to the treatment of obsessional slowness.

At this point it might be instructive to provide Mrs. C.'s firsthand account of undergoing treatment for obsessions and compulsions. This should prove helpful to the therapist in understanding what the patient feels and illustrate some of the fears and problems encountered in conducting the treatment. It should be noted that we deviated to some extent from our normal program with this patient to try to satisfy scheduling difficulties. In addition, her disorder was moderately severe but was deemed to be less severe than those of many of the patients in our clinic.

FIRST PERSON DESCRIPTION
BY MRS. C.

When I went for treatment at WPIC I was apprehensive. I wondered what could be done for me. I was somewhat hopeful, but I did not want to get my hopes up too high and then be disappointed and discouraged if the treatment didn't work for me. At my first appointment, Dr. Turner explained to me that I could be helped. He told me I was a milder case than many of his patients, but I did not feel like a mild case. He explained that medication is sometimes used as part of treatment and that treatment would involve raising my anxiety level as high as possible and not carrying out my rituals. The end result would be that I would no longer feel the drive to clean in order to relieve my anxiety. When I no longer responded to my anxiety by carrying out the cleaning, I would not feel so compelled to clean. Dr. Turner told me that I would be very uncomfortable before I would improve. I was still skeptical about the treatment because I had been through so much, but I was willing to try anything.

When I went in for my first treatment session, Dr. Turner placed dog hair on my lap. I was told to touch it, but I couldn't do that. Then he picked up my hand and placed it on the dog hair. I was very upset, anxious, and teary. This was very hard for me. While I was sitting there, Dr. Turner told me to imagine going home and not washing my hands or anything I touched. I was to imagine touching light switches, doorknobs, walls, everything without washing my hands first. I could only wash before eating. It is important to say here that if I had been permitted to shower and wash after I had gone home, I would not have experienced so much distress. My anxiety did go down after a while, but I had such strong feelings of contamination. I didn't even want to touch the door handle of the car. I stopped for lunch on the way home, and that's when I washed my hands. One thing I was able to overcome was washing the bottoms of my shoes. I hung up my coat, sweater and skirt at home and felt like they were contaminated. I could not go through the house touching everything though. I had two more treatments like this, with some good results. I no longer had to wash groceries that I brought home or wash the children's toys or other things I bought at the store.

For the next treatment, Dr. Turner brought in a dog. I had to touch it and let it walk around my legs. Even the smell of it bothered me. I was very anxious and upset, and the dog didn't like me either. I was not able to go through my house and touch everything as I had been instructed to do. At this point Dr. Turner told me he would be sending one of his interns to my house to help me because I was not able to touch everything in my house. I was very anxious over this. I called Dr. Turner and told him I didn't mean to be difficult but I just couldn't continue like this. That's when I was placed on Elavil. The dosage was increased two times at intervals of several weeks. With the first increase in dosage, I was able to think through my problems much better. I was able to have more confidence that the treatment would work. I was able to be more rational. I was also able to sleep at night.

However, I was still afraid of the intern's coming into my home and contaminating everything. I was afraid that after she left, I would be unable to live in my home without washing everything she had touched. I would never be able to live there, and I had nowhere else to go.

When I met the intern, Julie, I began to feel better. She was so warm and friendly and answered my questions. We talked for an hour. I asked her exactly what she would be doing. She said she would be there to help me. I asked her how she would help me. She told me she would help to complete the tasks. Then she said that the most important thing was not to wash or clean anything after she had gone. As we talked, my anxiety lifted. On my way home I stopped at a shopping mall and walked. As I walked, I began to feel a little more normal and that I could see beyond Saturday when Julie would be at my home. I began to feel that maybe it might all work out for me, that I would not have to feel this tremendous weight on me, that maybe I could come out from under it.

Throughout the next 3 days, I kept trying to convince myself that this treatment would work. I finally began to really feel it would work, and my confidence continued to grow. I was still very anxious and worried, but there was more hope and possibility present too. Something else had changed. I was now able to have people into the house without scrubbing and vacuuming the floors. I was finally believing that this was going to work for me. I was really glad to see Julie at my home.

We sat down at the kitchen table and talked for a while. Exactly what was said I can't remember. She did say she wanted me to show her through the house, which I did. I took her through every room in the house. Then we started in reverse order, only this time she started touching everything very slowly. I was told to follow behind and touch everything she touched. It was like we were spreading the contamination. She touched doorknobs, light switches, walls, pictures, and woodwork. She opened drawers in each bedroom and touched the contents. She opened closets and touched clothes hanging on the rods. She touched the towels and sheets in the linen closets. She went through the children's rooms, touching dolls, stuffed animals, models, Star Wars figures, Transformers, and books.

Julie kept talking to me quietly and calmly all the time we went along. I had been anxious when we started, but, as we continued, my anxiety level decreased. At one point, when I had begun to think the worst was over, she pointed to the attic door and said we were going inside. I said, "No, that's where the mice were." She told me I didn't want to have a place in my home that was off limits. I agreed but became very anxious again. I watched her go inside and walk around. She touched boxes and other items and told me to come inside too and begin touching the same things she was touching. It was very hard for me to go inside. I began

TOCD– F

touching the boxes too, but I was very upset. Then she put her hands down on the floor and wanted me to do the same. I said, "I can't. I just can't." Julie said, "Yes you can."

I thought about those mice running over the floor 2 years earlier. I was so anxious, but I wanted this to work for me. I finally touched the floor while Julie kept talking to me. We touched a few more boxes inside and left the attic. Julie touched the railing of the stairway. I thought to myself, "She's not really going to touch the clothes in my baby's dresser." But she did. Then I had to touch them too. We went all though the house two more times, touching everything as we had earlier. In the basement I had to touch the joists in the ceiling where the squirrel had been. I knew I would have been very anxious over touching the basement ceiling, but now nothing was as distressing as touching the floor in the attic, and I had made it through that.

Julie spent several hours with me that day. Before she left, she made a list of things for me to do by myself. Twice a day I was to go through the house touching everything the way she had done with me. I was to invite a friend of mine who had a pet to visit me and also friends of my children who had pets. I was to think about her coming back and bringing her dog along. Julie told me that the sooner I did these things, the easier they would be for me.

I wandered around the house looking at everything. I was feeling the contamination everywhere, but it wasn't unbearable. I kept wanting the treatment to work so much. I called my mother to tell her I had made it through the procedure. As I continued feeling everything was all right, I also felt like I had more and more energy. I wandered around the house not knowing exactly what to do. It was almost strange not having something somewhere in my house that I needed to wash. I looked at the piano keys and thought of touching them after being in the attic. I thought about just washing them, just that one thing; but then, because I wanted the treatment to work so much, I didn't wash them. I finally sat down at the piano and played sheet music for 2 hours. When I went to bed that night, I slept, and I had not cleaned anything.

The next day I was restless, almost bursting with energy, and I decided to run outside. I felt like I was receiving oxygen. I could breathe so easily and so deeply in the cold, crisp air. Everything around me was white, and I could feel the snowflakes on my face. As I passed one house, I heard a dog barking. I looked over my shoulder and saw it running toward me. I immediately tensed up at the thought that it would jump on me and get dog hair on me. Then I realized my compulsion was over and I did not have to worry about that anymore. It was terrific!

It was now easy for me to go through my house and attic every day touching everything the same way Julie had done with me. I never would have believed I could do this. I enjoyed having my friends come to the house again without having to watch everything they touched or wash and clean everything in the house afterward. It was such a relief to just enjoy people again. Julie kept in touch with me by phone over the next few months to see how I was doing. I also continued to see Dr. Turner.

Two months later Dr. Turner was still reminding me that the only way to further decrease the fear would be to bring an animal into my house. I made arrangements with a friend to borrow her cat. I left it in the kitchen and family room and even played with it and enjoyed it the same as when I was a little girl. I never would have believed this part would be so easy.

The hardest part of my experience was the exposure treatments at Dr. Turner's office and then in my home. What Julie called anticipatory anxiety was also hard for me. I was always worried about what would happen to me next, about how much distress I would have to experience next. There was also the despair of knowing that the treatment might not work for me, that I might have to live with feeling like my whole house was contaminated, and I would not have any place to go. My hysteria was also hard to deal with, but they helped me through that too.

SUMMARY

We have attempted to provide a reasonable clinical description of the behavioral treatment program used in the WPIC Anxiety Disorders Clinic for the treatment of obsessive–compulsive patients. In doing so, we have highlighted some of the clinical nuances encountered when using behavioral treatments, as well as in managing patients with an obsessional state. Naturally, we have not touched upon every possibility. We believe a critical factor to be noted is that in order to use these treatments properly, adequate training in the use of the treatments, basic understanding of their theoretical underpinnings, and knowledge of the psychopathology of obsessive–compulsive disorder is required. What we have described is the basic strategy used to bring the disorder under control. In chapter 7, we will describe the necessary program for maintaining treatment gains and increasing the likelihood of further improvement.

Chapter 5

Implementing Behavioral
Treatment Strategies

Constructing an appropriate intervention strategy requires considerable thought, knowledge of the theoretical underpinnings of the behavioral strategies to be employed, knowledge of the psychopathology of OCD, and, more often than not, considerable creativity. To give clinicians a better understanding of how we actually implement treatment, we have included some specific programs that were used to treat obsessional patients in our clinic. A brief description of the problem will be presented in each instance, followed by the behaviors targeted for direct intervention. Also, there will be a commentary at the end of each case.

Although most of the treatment plans to be presented were based on inpatient cases, with minimal alteration they can be adapted for outpatients. These plans are presented as examples of interventions for specific problematic behaviors; obviously they do not represent the full range of interventions offered to any individual patient. It must be remembered that an individualized treatment strategy should be developed for each patient. Thus, the treatment plans presented here should not be considered for use with other patients. Also, in describing the cases, we do not provide a comprehensive account of the patients' condition. Of course, all programs are explained fully to the patients before they are instituted, and they are instituted only with the patients' full consent.

EXAMPLE 1

Problem

The patient experienced continuous anxiety, obsessional thoughts related to fear of injuring or harming others, and a feeling of persistent need to check various objects in his environment.

Description of the Problem

For the past several years, the patient had been unable to drive a car, due to the persistent fear that he might run over someone, particularly a child. Similarly, whenever walking, he felt the need to check and recheck to be sure he had not stepped on someone, bumped anyone, or in any way caused an injury. He further described his disorder as characterized by the need to check underneath various items such as plates on the table, shampoo, and toothpaste, despite the fact that he was unsure as to what he was actually looking for. His days were characterized by a wide variety of checking behaviors including a set ritual that he had to go through each morning on arising and numerous rituals associated with bathing and getting ready for work. Similarly, at work, he felt the need to check and recheck and was unable to discard work-related material that was no longer useful. In addition, he had washing rituals associated with the fear that he might somehow contaminate others, although there was apparently no specific contaminant.

Treatment Plan

1. *Baseline (3 days).* No restrictions on behavior except that the patient should be out of his room as much as possible. The staff should tally the number of checking behaviors that occur within the first 15 minutes of every hour without intervening in his checking behavior. See list of checking behaviors for examples.
2. *Intervention:* Exposure and response prevention were decided on. *Response prevention* means that the unit staff will intervene in all of the patient's attempts to check. The staff will need to watch the patient closely to determine when he is about to engage in checking behavior; as he attempts to do so, the staff member should say in a loud, firm voice, "Stop!" and then redirect the patient to another activity. Other possibly effective techniques are distraction, discussion of a neutral topic, cajoling, and, occasionally mild, physical prompting. DO NOT ATTEMPT TO RESTRAIN THE PATIENT PHYSICALLY IF HE BECOMES INDIGNANT OR PHYSICALLY RESISTS. Response prevention should occur at all times while the patient is awake. The following restrictions are to be placed on the patient's washing behaviors: He is allowed a maximum of 10 minutes to shower each day, 10 minutes to use the sink (shave, wash hands, brush teeth) in the morning, and a maximum of 15 minutes to change out of pajamas and get dressed. This is to prevent checking or excessive washing. If any of the behaviors are not completed within the time limits, they are to be left undone for that day.

Checking behaviors
1. Lifting objects to look underneath them (during daily showers and at other times).
2. Requesting information about health and possible injury to people with whom patient has come in contact or returning to check on their whereabouts or health.
3. Returning to a place he has just left to look at or check an object (Example: Returns to bathroom to check toilet handle).
4. Looking over his shoulder as he walks (to see if he has caused an injury).
5. Reading the newspaper or watching TV news to check for reports of injuries that he has caused.
6. Making telephone calls to police or relatives to find out if he has injured anyone.

Exposure situations
The purpose of *exposure* is to confront the patient with feared situations. When exposure occurs, anxiety is likely to increase, and then, over time, decrease. Once every 15 minutes during the day (except at group times and mealtimes while he is eating), the staff should expose the patient to situations he usually avoids or in which he spends a great deal of time checking. The staff must prevent the patient from engaging in any checking behaviors. Listed next are typical exposure situations. More situations can be added as they become evident.

On the inpatient unit
1. Walk the patient up and down the halls, encouraging him to make eye contact with people he passes but preventing him from looking over his shoulder or asking for information about whether he has injured anyone.
2. Have the patient shake hands with staff members in nurses' station but prevent him from returning to check for injuries.
3. Have the patient open and walk through doors.
4. Have the patient walk to dayroom at the other end of the hall, walk him around the dayroom, then return him to his own room. Prevent him from checking back with people he passed or from talking about his fear of hurting someone.
5. Arrange for several staff members to bump into the patient at different times as he walks down the hall. The staff members should leave the area quickly. The accompanying staff member should refuse to answer questions about injuries and should prevent the patient from following the bumped person.
6. Encourage the patient to bump into preplaced staff members as he walks down the hall, as treatment progresses. Bumped staff member should quickly leave the area.

7. Have the patient, on days when he has been off the unit for exposure sessions (a) upon return, sit near the television during the noon and evening news, but hold a conversation with him so that he cannot attend to what the reporters are saying; (b) take a copy of the newspaper, but prevent him from reading the front page or news sections.

Off the unit
1. Take the patient on walks or for driving sessions. These sessions will occur on a daily basis until further notice.

Commentary

This patient presented with a multitude of washing and checking rituals. A program of response prevention and flooding was instituted immediately after completion of behavioral assessment. The response-prevention program included setting reasonable time limits for daily hygiene activities, so that the patient was permitted to shower each day but did not have enough time to complete these activities should he begin to perform any rituals. The exposure program for this patient focused on contact with others (e.g., shaking hands, bumping into someone) to address his fear of causing injury. No specific program to address his secondary contamination fears was instituted, as he was never able to identify specific contaminants. These concerns were fairly vague, and, in fact, remitted when the more primary fears were addressed. Additional treatment was required on an outpatient basis for this patient.

The descriptions of response prevention and exposure provided in this example were routinely given to all staff members involved in the patient's care. Thus, they are physically included in every treatment plan. However, for the sake of brevity, they will not be repeated in subsequent examples. It should be noted that close supervision of the inpatient staff was required on a daily basis.

EXAMPLE 2

Problem

Obsessional thoughts concerning fears of illness or injury to self through physical activity resulted in severe restriction of ambulatory activities for the patient.

Description of Problem

Upon admission to the hospital, the patient reported that she had always been fearful of germs and pain and that her friends had often called her a hypochondriac. She described herself as an "exercise nut" and engaged in some sort of exercise on a daily basis. Six years ago, she had injured her Achilles tendon while playing tennis and reportedly became clinically depressed because of the subsequent restrictions on her physical activity. The injury healed, but the patient perceived a continuing tingling sensation, for which she sought many medical consultations. She also resumed her vigorous exercise program. Six months before admission, the patient had bruised her other leg in an aerobics class and, since that time, she had had an increasing number of intrusive thoughts about injuring herself more seriously and of becoming a cripple. At the time of admission, she refused to walk up or down steps, open doors, bend over, or walk any distance, due to her fears of permanent injury. She also had discontinued all forms of exercise, which was a source of great distress. She had become obsessed with finding the "right" pair of shoes which would provide comfort and support and prevent injury. Since the time of her second injury, she had become increasingly withdrawn and described decreased interest in activities; decreased libido; decreased energy; decreased appetite, with a 20-lb weight loss; decreased sleep, with difficulty falling asleep; sleep continuity disturbance; and early morning awakening. Her mood had been sad, and she had suicidal ideation but no attempts.

Behaviors Targeted for Intervention

1. Avoids wearing any shoes other than bedroom slippers or will change shoes every 2 hours to prevent any one pair of shoes from injuring her foot.
2. Avoids walking stairs, being particularly fearful of walking down stairs and of leading off with the right foot.
3. Avoids pulling open any door.
4. Avoids walking fast.
5. Avoids walking on other than level, paved surfaces, being particularly fearful of walking down grassy, unpaved hills.
6. Avoids stooping, bending, or lying on stomach face down.
7. Spends significant amount of time (8 hours per week) in shoe stores, examining and testing shoes for fit, comfort, and safety, but does not buy any shoes or boots.
8. Spends 4 hours per day checking her calves and feet for possibility of injury.
9. Continuously seeks reassurance from husband and medical personnel about the extent of her past injuries and implications for future functioning.

Initial Treatment Plan

Due to the presence of the depressive symptoms, antidepressant medication was prescribed immediately. Once the medication had reached a therapeutic level and the patient reported improvement in sleep, appetite, and general level of functioning, the following behavioral plan was implemented.

1. The patient brought nine pairs of shoes and a pair of bedroom slippers to the hospital. All shoes and slippers are to be removed from her room. Each morning, a nurse will select one pair of shoes for her to wear. She will wear those shoes until bedtime.
2. She is to go on extended walks, accompanied by a staff person, once per day (flooding sessions). She is to wear the shoes designated for that day and is not allowed to change into sneakers or bedroom slippers for the flooding sessions. The course to be walked should be selected by the accompanying staff member and should include as many unpaved roads, hills, rutted areas, and stairs as possible. The flooding sessions shall be conducted under all the usual guidelines set forth by the Anxiety Disorders Clinic.
3. She should be required to use the stairs as often as possible, inside the hospital.
4. Staff members are to refrain from answering any questions concerning the possibility of injury from engaging in any of the listed activities. This includes direct questioning or responding to comments such as "My leg is really getting sore."
5. The patient is to refrain from checking her legs or feet for injury. The staff is to prevent such checking activities if the patient appears unable to do so or if she asks for help.

Revised Treatment Plan

This should be added approximately 10 days after the initial program is instituted, at the discretion of the Anxiety Disorders Clinic staff.

1. All of the patient's shoes will be returned to her. The staff will still designate one pair of shoes she is to wear at all times while awake until further notice. No substitutions will be allowed.
2. The patient will be escorted to a shoe store to buy one pair of boots for the winter season. The following constraints will be placed on the visit:
   a. The patient will be accompanied by a staff member.
   b. The patient will be allowed 10 minutes to look over the shoe display and decide if there are any boots she would like to try on. This decision must be based on visual inspection only. She will not touch

the shoes in any way. If, after 10 minutes, she has made no decision, she will have to leave the store.

c. The patient will be given 10 minutes to try on any boots she selects to test. At the end of the 10-minute period, she must either make a purchase or leave the store.

d. The patient may go to only two stores in the area.

3. The patient is required to lie in a prone position on the bed for a 5-minute period each day. She must keep her shoes on, and all parts of her feet must be on the bed.

4. The patient is required to use the exercise bicycle for 15 minutes each day.

5. During group therapy sessions, the patient is not to discuss her medical condition or any reasons why she might have developed this disorder. A more appropriate topic for discussion would be problems related to her job.

These interventions will be conducted on a daily basis (with the exception of shopping for boots) and will remain in effect until self-monitoring data indicate elimination or a substantial decrease in obsessions and compulsions.

Commentary

The exposure situations in this treatment plan were somewhat similar to those in Example 1, yet the fear had a very different basis. In this example, the fear was of injury to self rather than to others. This treatment plan illustrates an important point: To get certain symptoms under control, it is sometimes necessary to exert a great deal of control over the patient's environment and then give the responsibility back to the patient in small increments. For example, the patient's shoes were a source of considerable distress to her. In addition to feeling compelled to change them every 2 hours, she felt that none of them were actually suitable for her needs. Furthermore, all of the shoes were very expensive. Thus, their constant presence was a source of considerable distress, not only in trying to resist the compulsion, but as a constant reminder of all the money she had "wasted" on "unsuitable" shoes. Therefore, the patient's shoes were initially removed from her room to prevent engagement in any rituals and to temporarily decrease her distress. Once the exposure program had been instituted and was beginning to show some effectiveness, the shoes were returned to the patient's room. She was still not permitted to select any shoes, thus alleviating her concern about choosing the "wrong" shoes. With further treatment, there was less concern about injury from wearing the wrong shoes and in the final phase prior to discharge, responsibility for shoe selection was returned to the patient.

EXAMPLE 3

Problem

The patient described obsessional thoughts related to fear of contamination by others, extensive and ritualistic washing behaviors, and avoidance of educational and social activities.

Description of Problem

The patient described a long-standing fear of contamination from germs associated with "dirty children at school." Initially, she had avoided these children but starting in high school these fears became more intense and generalized to an increasing number of children. She began to engage in handwashing and cleaning upon return from school. Subsequently, she began to throw away clothing she had worn to school and to use abrasive cleaners to wash herself. She dropped out of school the next year because of these fears. In addition, she withdrew socially and terminated housebound school instruction because she feared that the work materials were contaminated and the housebound instructor's presence contaminated her home. She was essentially housebound during the following year and developed symptoms of secondary depression characterized by dysphoria, irritability, difficulty falling asleep, and feelings of hopelessness. There was also a history of alcohol abuse on a daily basis (up to one bottle of wine) for the year preceding her coming to the clinic. She had been treated with several tricyclic antidepressant medications but to no avail.

Treatment Plan

This consisted of in vivo exposure and response prevention.

Exposure situations
1. The patient's family will contaminate a towel with "dirt" from the family home. They will also secure contaminated items from the patient's school. The towel and objects will be brought to the clinic for flooding sessions, where the patient will handle these objects in the presence of the clinician. These exposure sessions will occur on a daily basis.

2. The patient initially will spend a minimum of 1½ hours per day in a part of her home that she feels is contaminated. At the discretion of the therapist, this time will be gradually increased.

3. The patient will renew social contacts with her friends. First, she will visit friends who attend high schools other than her own. At a later point (again at the discretion of the therapist), she will visit friends who attend the same high school. These visits will last at least 2 hours.

4. The patient, in the company of her parents, will go to her high school and stay on the school grounds for a minimum of 1½ hours. These visits will take place when school is not in session. At a later date, the patient will enroll in a summer school class offered by the high school and will attend the class every day.

5. The patient will return to her high school at the beginning of the fall semester. She will attend regular classes for a half day and receive special tutoring to make up missed work from not attending the year before.

Response prevention

1. The patient will not take a shower until at least 1½ hours after returning home from any clinic flooding session or any homework assignment where she has had to be in contact with contaminated objects. This includes visiting her friends and her school or being in any part of her home that she feels is contaminated.

2. The patient will be limited to one shower per day for a duration of 10 minutes. During that time, she must bathe and if she wishes to do so, wash her hair. Showering and shampooing must be completed using a mild bar soap and a commercial shampoo, not an abrasive cleanser.

3. The patient will limit handwashing to 30 seconds and be done only before meals or after using the lavatory.

4. The patient will not throw away clothing that has been in contact with contaminated objects. She will launder it once, using a regular laundry detergent.

Commentary

This treatment plan was very successful in eliminating ritualistic behavior and decreasing obsessional thoughts. This patient lived quite some distance from the Anxiety Disorders Clinic, yet was willing to travel that distance daily to get treatment. After a careful evaluation of the family situation and due to the distance and patient's age (below 18), it was decided that the parents would have to play an active role in the treatment plan, first as procurers of contaminated articles and later as "assistant therapists." In this fashion, the therapist's time could be spent on the actual flooding session and did not have to be spent traveling great distances to carry out exposure sessions at the patient's school. The family was supportive of treatment and willing to carry out the instructions of the therapist. It is important to note that, at first, the family was limited to a support role. That is, they obtained contaminated objects and assisted in response prevention; they did not conduct flooding sessions without the clinician's presence until the disorder was under some control. They never conducted flooding sessions without direct instructions from the clinician.

A second important point is that this program was not completely effective in eliminating the obsessions. After the patient returned to school, she continued to come to the clinic (on a less frequent basis) and was instructed in the use of thought-stopping. This procedure appeared to have a further effect on reducing obsessional thinking.

EXAMPLE 4

Problem

The patient's obsessional thoughts concerning the possible occurrence of thunderstorms, accompanied by continuous monitoring of weather reports and TV weather channels, culminated in various avoidance behaviors such as refusing to drive or leave home on cloudy days or when there was a threat of rain.

Description of Problem

The patient reported that his fears had begun several years ago, after a flash flood occurred in his hometown. This flood washed out his driveway but did not damage his house or the rest of his grounds. Nonetheless, the patient reported that since that time, he had repetitive, intrusive thoughts concerning the possibility of another thunderstorm and resultant flood. He watched the weather channel whenever he was home and refused to drive anywhere if there was a report of or threat of rain in the general area. During a storm, he looked out of all of his windows in a certain fashion to check for the possibility of a flood, he stood on his porch for long periods of time to observe the road for water, and he went out into the storm to a small stream located near his driveway to monitor the water level. If it was night, he would use a flashlight to check the water level, and he would often stand in the rain for a long period of time, just watching the water. If there was a threat of a storm at night, he would sleep on the living room sofa, in order to monitor the storm. Finally, he reported increased anxiety whenever it became cloudy, as well as during darkness.

Treatment Plan

Due to the unpredictable nature of thunderstorms, an imaginal flooding paradigm rather than an in vivo program was instituted. Flooding sessions were conducted on a daily basis for 12 days. The following scene was constructed, based on patient self-report and information obtained via interview.

Flooding Scene You are mowing your lawn in the early afternoon. It is a hot, sticky day, almost 90 degrees. You remember that the morning weather report and the morning paper predicted afternoon thunderstorms. As you glance at the sky, you notice it is beginning to become cloudy; there are very high white clouds in the sky. You notice a slight twinge in your stomach as you continue to mow the lawn.

When you glance at the sky again, you see that it is becoming darker and large thunderclouds are forming. You rush inside and turn on the weather channel. It has become so dark now that you must turn on a light to see. The weather channel announces a "severe thunderstorm warning" for your part of the state. The meteorologist adds that further to the west there has been some flooding and there is the potential for floods where you live. You remember that the ground is already saturated from yesterday's rain and the chance for flooding today is good. At the same time, you notice the rumble of thunder off in the distance. Your stomach feels as if it is tied up in knots, and you notice that you feel more uneasy. (At this point in the narration, thunderstorm sounds, taped from a thunderstorm sound effects record, are introduced, and these sounds continue to play throughout the rest of the flooding session.)

You remember the devastation from the last flood and wonder if it will happen again today. Suddenly, there is a brilliant flash of light, followed by a loud crack of lightning. You look out the window and see that the wind is blowing hard. Then it thunders, and the house appears to be shaking from the noise. You wonder if the storm will stall over your area or move through fast. Your stomach is in knots and feels upset, and you are having difficulty concentrating on anything but the storm.

It starts to rain; lightly at first, then really coming down hard. All of a sudden, you realize all of your windows are open because it was such a hot, sticky day. You race upstairs and close them all and then downstairs to close the downstairs windows. Your heart is beating fast now from climbing the stairs, and you are a little out of breath.

You look out your front window, and it is raining very hard, so hard that you can barely see the creek gully or the highway. You think about the blueberry bushes where the water always seems to collect first.

You hear the rain pounding on the windows and the porch. You know the rain is filling up parts of the yard and flowing toward the creek. You wonder if the creek will be able to hold the water from this intense storm. Maybe the pipe you put under the driveway after the last storm is not large enough to prevent another flood. You strain to see the creek gully, but it is still raining too hard to see it clearly. You look at your watch and realize it has been raining a long time now. You worry that the storm will not pass quickly but will stall. You hear another loud clap of thunder. They seem to be occurring very frequently now, which means the storm is not letting up.

You were thinking about going to the store before dinner, but, with this storm, you know you will not be able to go out. You turn to the weather channel, and there is a report of a severe thunderstorm warning for your area for the next 3 hours. The reporter also mentions that flooding has occurred in areas very close to you.

You look out your front door, and you see water just cascading off the roof. It is coming down like a waterfall. You can hear the rain hitting the puddles in your driveway. It continues to rain very hard. Even though it is a summer afternoon, it is so dark that you have to turn on the lights. You can really feel the heat and humidity. The sky is entirely dark; there are no clear skies on the horizon. You can hear the water rushing out over the gutters. They are so full, they cannot take all the water that is pouring out of the sky.

It continues to thunder and lightning. You imagine that the water flowing toward the creek is quite brown now. You think about checking the creek, but you know there is nothing you can do. If it floods, nothing can stop it. You wonder how long this storm can last.

Another crack of thunder comes from up on the hill. It was very close and loud. It must have hit something the way that it sounded. You remember the last time it rained so hard some water leaked in through the basement window, but you do not go down to check it. The storm just continues. (Continue exposure, repeating the narration of the scene, ending the session according to the Anxiety Disorders Clinic guidelines.)

In vivo exposure After 12 days of imaginal flooding, the inpatient staff should be prepared for the possibility of upcoming thunderstorms. Should a thunderstorm occur, take the patient to the front of the building or into the parking garage. Allow him to be protected from the weather yet be as close to being in the thunderstorm as possible, within all the usual guidelines for safety during electrical storms. Keep him there for the duration of the thunderstorm, and do not reassure him about the possibility of flooding at his home.

Discharge Treatment Plan

This is given to the patient at discharge.
The following plan is to be instituted when you go home:
1. Do not watch the weather channel.
2. Do not sleep downstairs when a storm is predicted, but sleep in your own bedroom.
3. During a thunderstorm: (a) sit in one place and do *not* walk to other rooms in the house to check the storm; (b) become involved in an activity that will distract you from the storm (e.g., conversation, cards, watching TV); (c) during the first 2 or 3 storms, it is recommended that family members come over and help distract you from the storm.
4. Call the clinic immediately after the first thunderstorm.

Commentary

This case presented several challenges for the clinician. First, the stimuli could not be controlled, as we might have wished. It was impossible to use real thunderstorms because of their unpredictability and unlikelihood of daily occurrence. Thus, an imaginal scene had to be constructed. This scene could be used on a daily basis, and, should an actual thunderstorm occur, we could incorporate that into the program as well.

The construction and presentation of the scene were crucial. A detailed assessment included a description of the patient's house and yard, and images he could readily recall. The use of somatic cues was also important in assisting the patient to imagine these events. The terminology used ("stomach in knots") were the patient's own words, the use of which served to increase realism. In the scene, all of the relevant cues were presented, but the patient was not permitted to engage in any of the rituals, nor to imagine engaging in them. This last point is particularly critical in that imagining the ritual, like actually performing it, decreases the patient's anxiety, thus being counterproductive to the intent of the flooding session. Clinicians must be vigilant, so that the patient does not engage in these avoidance maneuvers.

We also have included a written discharge plan with this example. This is another standard part of our intervention, particularly for patients who live at great distances from our clinic and who will not be returning for outpatient follow-up care. The discharge instructions provided for continuity of care until outpatient treatment in his home could be instituted.

EXAMPLE 5

Problem

The patient engaged in compulsive exercise.

Description of the Problem

The patient reported that she felt compelled to exercise in a very rigid fashion. She had a specific expercise plan that included the time and place, as well as the specific exercise and the number of repetitions. If she were interrupted, she became very angry and anxious and had to begin again.

Treatment Plan

Three times per day (morning, afternoon, and evening), staff should instruct the patient to begin exercising. The staff will choose the place for the exercise and the specific exercise to be performed. The exact time of the exercise should be varied, and the patient should not be informed about the time until the session is to begin. During each exercise session, the total time spent exercising should be no longer than 15 minutes, and the patient should be observed throughout the exercise period. At some point during the 15-minute period, she should be interrupted and told to stop exercising. The exact time of the interruption should be varied with each session. Once she has stopped exercising, she should not be allowed to exercise until the next exercise session is to begin.

Commentary

The goal of most behavioral interventions with OCD patients is to eliminate rituals, reduce obsessive ideation, and reduce anxiety level. In this case, the goal was not to eliminate exercising, but only to eliminate engagement in this activity in a compulsive, rigid fashion. Therefore, the program was designed to allow the patient to exercise but at the same time prevent the behavior from being carried out in a compulsive fashion.

SUMMARY

The above case examples were provided to illustrate how response prevention and flooding were used to treat a number of patients with different patterns of obsessions and compulsions. Although the goal was the same in each instance (to prevent the occurrence of rituals and extinguish anxiety and obsessional ideation), the manner in which we proceeded was different for each case. This illustrates a number of points we have repeatedly emphasized throughout this book. *First*, no one strategy of implementation is suitable for every patient. Thus, an individual treatment plan is necessary in each case. *Second*, the therapist must be knowledgeable about the disorder. *Third*, the therapist must not only be familiar with the technical aspects of the behavioral treatments, but also must be familiar with the theoretical model on which they are based. Perusal of these few cases clearly shows how differently the strategies were used. We hope these examples convey the complexity of the treatments and the time commitment that is required to effectively treat obsessional patients.

Chapter 6
Biological Treatment Strategies

As we noted in chapter 1, the clinical picture of obsessive–compulsive disorder includes symptoms of anxiety, unusual thinking, and depression. Pharmacological agents that have been useful in treating these symptoms in other psychiatric disorders have also been administered to OCD patients. In this chapter, we will address the role of drugs in the treatment of obsessive–compulsive disorder and the classes of medication used (antianxiety, antipsychotic, and antidepressant compounds). It is beyond the scope of this book to review all of the literature on the use of pharmacological interventions in obsessive–compulsive disorder. Rather, we will limit our discussion to the most recent findings involving drugs that have been most widely used. The reader is referred to appropriate review papers for more extensive coverage. Finally, we will briefly note other biological treatments, again referring the reader to primary sources for extended discussion.

ANTIANXIETY AGENTS

Due to the presence of severe anxiety, which accompanies the clinical picture of OCD, anxiolytic compounds often have been prescribed. These include commonly used drugs such as valium and librium, as well as the newer high-potency benzodiazepines such as alprazolam. In our clinic, patients who previously have been treated are frequently on various medications including anxiolytic agents. In general, we have found such drugs to have limited utility in the treatment of obsessional disorder. They also carry the risk of psychological and physiological addiction. Thus, patients in our clinic are normally withdrawn from these medications prior to initiation of treatment.

Evidence of the effectiveness of anxiolytics, particularly the more recent high-potency benzodiazepines such as alprazolam and clonazepam have received some support in the literature for effectiveness in the treatment of panic and agoraphobia (Rickels & Schweizer, 1986). With respect to OCD, Tesar and Jenike (1984) described the successful use of alprazolam in an OCD patient who had a prior history of panic attacks and episodic anxiety. The obsessions centered around the possibility that the patient might do something self-injurious. Treatment with 12 mg per day of alprazolam was reported to be successful in decreasing the obsessions, although no formal assessment strategy was used. It is unclear from the clinical description if the panic attacks were continuous with the obsessionality. If the panic attacks fueled the fear of losing control, which in turn contributed to the obsessions, then it is likely that the obsessions decreased as a result of the drug's blocking the panic attacks. Therefore, it is unclear that alprazolam had a direct anti-obsessional effect.

In 1976, Ananth reviewed the literature on the use of anxiolytic agents in OCD patients. He concluded that, although they had been found effective in decreasing the patient's physiological arousal, they were ineffective in decreasing either subjective feelings of anxiety or primary symptoms of obsessions and compulsions. Over a decade later, little further evidence has been put forth to challenge this conclusion.

NEUROLEPTIC AGENTS

Several investigators have examined the possibility of a relationship between OCD and other disorders such as Tourette's syndrome, Parkinson's disease, and schizophrenia (Pauls et al., 1986; S. M. Turner, Beidel, & Nathan, 1985). Indeed, there are certain symptoms of Tourette's syndrome and schizophrenia, which we touched upon in chapter 2, that are similar to obsessions and compulsions and that on the surface might suggest that neuroleptic medication, effective in treating the former disorders, might also be useful in the treatment of OCD. For example, individuals with Tourette's syndrome often display stereotypic, repetitive movements they describe as being outside of their control. Patients with schizophrenia report unusual thinking, specifically of a delusional nature, whereas a subgroup of OCD patients report the presence of overvalued ideation. There are several differences between these disorders and OCD, however. *First*, the stereotypic behavior of Tourette's syndrome consists mainly of tics and other involuntary body movements whereas the repetitive behavior of the OCD patient seems much more complex and involves self-selection. *Second*, in the case of Tourette's syndrome and schizophrenia, dopaminergic abnormalities have been documented whereas in OCD they have not. In addition, in the case of these disorders, it is not the same dopaminergic dysfunction. To our knowledge there have been no studies investigating dopaminergic functioning in OCD (S. M. Turner, Beidel, & Nathan, 1985). In addition, it has been our clinical experience that neuroleptic medication is ineffective in treating obsessions and compulsions, which could underscore the contention that altered levels of dopamine do not play a role in this condition. Finally, although one can make a case for considering overvalued ideation a delusion, these individuals do not necessarily appear to have other psychotic features. Nevertheless, as discussed in chapter 2, recent reports regarding the presence of schizotypal features in some OCD patients have led to the speculation that neuroleptics might have some beneficial effect in at least a subgroup (Jenike et al., 1986). However, empirical studies will need to be conducted to confirm this speculation. At the present, there is little empirical support for the use of neuroleptics in OCD. Given the potential for serious side effects of neuroleptic compounds and the lack of empirical support for their effectiveness, their use with OCD should probably be restricted to those cases that have not responded to other treatments or those that appear to have psychotic or schizotypal features.

ANTIDEPRESSANTS

There is some evidence for an association between obsessive–compulsive disorder and depression (e.g., S. M. Turner, Beidel, & Nathan, 1985). As we noted in chapters 1 and 2, many OCD patients have clinically significant symptoms of depression. In addition, Insel and his colleagues (e.g., Insel, Mueller, Alterman, Linnoila, & Murphy, 1985) have reported some similarities on sleep variables and dexamethasone suppression test responses in patients with major depression and obsessive–compulsive disorder. Treatment of OCD patients with tricyclic antidepressants such as amitriptyline and imipramine has been effective in decreasing the dysphoric mood states of these patients (Ananth, 1985), and as we shall discuss later in this chapter, could be an important aspect of the total treatment regimen. One concern, however, is whether these medications function merely to alleviate depressed mood or whether they have a specific anti-obsessional effect.

One of the actions of antidepressant medications is to affect the available levels of two neurotransmitters, norepinephrine and serotonin. Depletion of functional levels of these neurotransmitters has been associated with depressed mood, and one action of the antidepressants is to block the re-uptake of these transmitters at the neural synapse, thereby allowing them to remain in the synapse and be available for neurotransmission. Different compounds have differential effects on levels of norepinephrine and serotonin, with some compounds affecting one neurotransmitter much more than another. Of all the antidepressants, those that have created the most excitement in the treatment of obsessive–compulsive disorder are those with the most potent serotonergic action.

In 1977, Yaryura-Tobias proposed a serotonin hypothesis for obsessive–compulsive disorder, that OCD patients have decreased functional levels of serotonin available at the synaptic clefts. This finding prompted the increased use of drugs with potent serotonergic effects to treat OCD. The effectiveness of four compounds (trazodone, zimelidine, fluoxetine, and clomipramine) has been assessed in OCD patients, although only trazodone and fluoxetine are currently approved for general use in the United States.

Baxter (1985) published case reports of two OCD patients who had been unsuccessfully treated with a variety of antidepressants before being given a trial of trazodone. Although no formal assessments were conducted, both patients were reported to have significantly improved following treatment with this medication. Rituals were reported to have decreased, but they were not eliminated. In a second study, Prasad (1986) administered a 4-week trial of trazodone to 8 obsessional patients who were described as refractory to behavioral treatments. Ratings of symptomatology were made at pre- and posttreatment using the Leyton Obsessional Inventory and the Montgomery-Asberg Scale for Depression. It is unclear if the ratings were conducted by a blind interviewer, but the patients were not blind to their treatment status. Statistical analyses were not conducted but the data were presented in tabular form. According to the author, the patients who did not have high obsessional traits (as measured by the Leyton trait scores) tended to show improvement on the Leyton symptom ratings. These reports are encouraging and, as noted, trazodone is a drug that has effects on the serotonergic system. However, due to methodological shortcomings of these studies, firm conclusions about the efficacy of this drug in obsessional patients cannot be drawn. In our experience with this drug in our clinic, we have been disappointed and generally have found it to be among the least effective of the antidepressant agents.

Zimelidine is another selective serotonergic compound that has been tested with obsessive–compulsive patients. In an open trial, zimelidine was given to 6 OCD patients for an 8-week period (Kahn, Westenberg, & Jolles, 1984). Psychiatrist ratings of the patient on a symptom-specific rating scale indicated that 5 out of the 6 patients had a reduction in compulsive acts ranging from 50% to 100%. These findings appeared promising and encouraged the implementation of more sophisticated research designs. For example, Prasad (1984) conducted a double-blind study of imipramine versus zimelidine in 6 patients with OCD. All subjects received a 4-week trial of one of the medications. Symptoms were rated at pre- and posttreatment using the Leyton Inventory and the Montgomery-Asberg Scale for Depression. Both groups showed a reduction in level of depression but only the subjects who received zimelidine demonstrated a statistically significant reduction in obsessive–compulsive disorder, as measured by the Leyton Inventory. As noted by the author, these results are based on groups of three subjects each, and, therefore, the results must be interpreted cautiously. Insel and his colleagues have also examined the effect of zimelidine and compared it with those of other antidepressants, including clomipramine. The results of that study will be discussed in the section on clomipramine. Initially, the results with zimelidine appeared very promising. However, severe adverse reactions were experienced by individuals using this medication, including some deaths, and the drug has been withdrawn from use in the United States by the Food and Drug Administration.

Like zimelidine, fluoxetine was developed to have a neurochemical effect specifically for serotonin. The use of fluoxetine in the treatment of obsessive–compulsive disorder has also been the subject of two investigations. In an open clinic trial lasting 9 weeks, 7 outpatients with OCD were treated with fluoxetine (Fontaine & Chouinard, 1986). Patient improvement was rated on two psychiatric rating scales. After 9 weeks, the patients were judged to be significantly improved on both of these measures.

Fluoxetine also has been the subject of investigation employing tightly controlled single-case methodology. By use of a single-blind placebo design, the effects of a 12-week fluoxetine treatment program were investigated in a group of 10 OCD patients (S. M. Turner, Jacob, Beidel, & Himmelhoch, 1985). Self-report instruments, interviewer rating scales, and self-monitoring data were included in the assessment protocol. After 12 weeks of treatment there was significant improvement not only on depressive symptoms but also on the self-reported measures of obsessions and ritualistic behaviors. Although the drug did not completely eliminate the primary symptoms, there was a substantial decrease in the amount of time spent engaged in ritualizing and obsessional thinking. These improvements were not significantly correlated with pretreatment level of depression, although the lack of a statistically significant correlation could have been due to the small sample size. It remains our clinical impression that those OCD patients with the strongest affective component appeared to benefit the most from the medication. Following the discontinuation of medication at completion of the 3-month trial, five of these patients were given a 10-day trial of flooding and response prevention. Further improvements were noted, including decreased time spent ritualizing and obsessing, and a significantly decreased frequency of the obsessions and compulsive acts. Ten days of behavior therapy was judged to be more effective across all patients than 12 weeks of fluoxetine treatment. Side effects of this medication are thought to be minimal, although there have been two reports to our knowledge of hypomanic episodes developing concurrently with the use of fluoxetine (Settle & Settle, 1984; S. M. Turner, Jacob, Beidel, & Griffin, 1985). Fluoxetine recently has been approved for general clinical use. Again, the results are encouraging, but more extensive treatment studies are needed.

The antidepressant medication that has received the most attention and investigation is clomipramine. This drug, widely used in Europe and Canada, is only available for experimental and compassionate use in the United States. The effectiveness of this drug in treating OCD was discovered accidentally over 20 years ago (Ananth, 1986). Several recent reviews of the effectiveness of clomipramine in the treatment of obsessive–compulsive disorder are available, and the interested reader is referred to these for more detailed information (Ananth, 1983, 1986; Zohar & Insel, 1987).

Briefly, clomipramine has been the subject of numerous studies of patients with obsessive–compulsive disorder. The drug has been administered both orally and intravenously. Many of the studies are plagued by poor experimental design, lack of placebo controls, or omission of assessment instruments designed to specifically assess obsessions and compulsions separate from the related affective states of depression or anxiety. Therefore, although this drug has been considered to have anti-obsessional qualities, until very recently the research designs necessary to make this determination were not used. Zohar and Insel (1987) have calculated that the double-blind placebo-controlled studies have resulted in 106 OCD patients who have been administered clomipramine. In each of these studies clomipramine has been demonstrated to be superior to a placebo (Flament et al., 1985; Marks, Stern, Mawson, Cobb, & McDonald, 1980; Montgomery, 1980; Thoren, Asberg, Cronholm, Jornestedt, & Rachman, 1980). In the only negative report, Mawson, Marks, and Ramm (1982) compared the effect of 36 weeks of clomipramine or placebo but found no differences between the two groups at 1-year or 2-year follow-up. In this study, however, all of the patients also received at least 15 hours of in vivo exposure, and the effectiveness of the behavioral intervention might have washed out any comparative effects of the medications alone.

The efficacy of clomipramine has also been compared with that of other antidepressant medications such as imipramine, amitriptyline, and nortriptyline. Clomipramine was judged to be slightly superior to nortriptyline although not statistically significant (Thoren et al., 1980).

Ananth, Pecknold, Van Den Steen, and Engelsmann (1981) reported that clomipramine was effective in decreasing obsessions, depression, and anxiety, whereas amitriptyline was not. Volavka, Neziroglu, and Yaryura-Tobias (1985) found that clomipramine was slightly, but not significantly, more anti-obsessional than imipramine after a 12-week medication trial. Similar results were reported by Mavissakalian, Turner, Michelson, and Jacob (1985). In the Mavissakalian et al., study, both clomipramine and imipramine showed equivalent effectiveness on patient and clinician ratings of obsessions and compulsions. Insel and his colleagues (Insel, Mueller, Alterman, Linnoila, & Murphy, 1985) compared clomipramine to desipramine in a group of 28 obsessional patients. Assessment measures included observer ratings of depression and obsessive–compulsive symptoms. After 6 weeks of clomipramine treatment, both the most and least depressed patients were reported as improved. The most depressed patients had a 34% change from baseline in their Hamilton Depression score whereas the least depressed patients had a 58% decrease from baseline. In terms of OCD, the most depressed patients had a 24% improvement in symptom expression when compared with baseline. The least depressed reported a 34% improvement. In contrast, desipramine was not effective in decreasing OCD or improving affect.

In a more recent investigation, Zohar and Insel (1987) again compared clomipramine with desipramine in a group of OCD patients. This group of patients was carefully selected to have low initial levels of depression. The results of the study indicated that there were no differences between the groups on posttreatment measures of depression or overall distress. However, clomipramine was significantly superior to desipramine on observer ratings of obsessive–compulsive symptoms. As noted by the authors, the differences in improvement on OCD symptoms, although statistically significant, represented only a 28% improvement in their clinical condition. In a third investigation, clomipramine was compared with zimelidine and desipramine (Insel, Mueller, Gillin, et al., 1985). Following a placebo washout, patients were first randomly assigned to either zimelidine or desipramine for 5 weeks. Nonresponders completed a second 4-week placebo washout and then were administered clomipramine. There were no differences at posttreatment between the zimelidine and the desipramine groups on any of the assessment measures. In addition, there were no significant within-group differences on any of the variables for the zimelidine group. Clomipramine treatment however, resulted in significant improvement on observer ratings of global obsessive–compulsive symptoms, global impairment, and the Hamilton Rating Scale for Depression. The failure of zimelidine cannot be attributed to an ability to increase functional levels of serotonin as platelet and cerebrospinal fluid assessments documented the increases during zimelidine administration.

The failure of zimelidine, a potent serotonin agonist, to affect OCD presents some difficulties for the serotonin hypothesis. Obviously, if it were just a matter of increasing functional levels of serotonin, zimelidine should be just as effective as clomipramine in reducing obsessions and compulsions. The situation does not appear to be that simple, and part of the answer might lie in the unique characteristics of clomipramine's action. Thus, although clomipramine is fairly specific in its effect on serotonin, its major metabolite, desmethyl clomipramine, acts primarily on norepinephrine receptors. Coincidentally, imipramine, which appears to produce improvements similar to those achieved by clomipramine, has the identical chemical properties. As noted by Insel, Mueller, Alterman, et al. (1985), perhaps both noradrenergic and serotonin re-uptake blockade are necessary for an anti-obsessional effect. Ananth (1986) came to a similar conclusion when he proposed that clomipramine might be the anti-obsessive component and desmethyl clomipramine, the anti-depressive component. A second reason for the difference between the two drugs might have to do with the specific binding sites they affect. Zimelidine appears to bind more specifically to certain areas whereas clomipramine appears much less discriminant. This lack of specificity might contribute to its effectiveness, but these hypotheses await further investigation. For a more extensive discussion of serotonin and OCD, the interested reader is referred to Insel, Mueller, Alterman, et al. (1985).

OTHER PHARMACOLOGICAL AND BIOLOGICAL TREATMENTS

The psychiatric literature contains case reports of patients who have been treated with other medications such as lithium (Stern & Jenike, 1983), lithium and tryptophan augmentation (Rasmussen, 1984), and L-tryptophan (Yaryura-Tobias & Bhagavan, 1977). Some success has been reported with these regimens, but the fact that this literature is limited to case reports makes it difficult to assess their utility. Other treatments such as electroconvulsive therapy (ECT) and leukotomy also have been reported to be effective. The literature on ECT is limited to case reports and therefore cannot be the basis for broad generalizations. Leukotomies are only very rarely performed in the United States, although one report does indicate some effectiveness (Kelley, 1973). However, compared with medical and behavioral treatments, these interventions are invasive, could have irreversible side effects, and, given the high success rate for drugs and behavior therapy, are probably unnecessary.

THE USEFULNESS OF MEDICATION
IN THE TREATMENT OF OCD

Is there any drug that can be stated to have anti-obsessional qualities? Of all the medications, it appears that clomipramine, and possibly imipramine, are the most anti-obsessive compounds currently available for clinical use. Fluoxetine might be equally effective but it will require several replication trials before its potential can be firmly established. It should be noted, however, that clomipramine's action appears to work by suppressing the symptoms rather than eliminating them. Withdrawal of the medication precipitates a relapse in up to 70% of the patients treated with this drug (Ananth, 1986). In addition, although clomipramine appears to be superior to currently available antidepressant medications in terms of observer ratings of decreases in obsessions and compulsions, the improvement ratings range from between 28% and 34%. This can hardly be considered an outstanding effect. Furthermore, data from more than just observer rating scales are needed. Changes on established psychometric self-report scales and self-monitoring data would be useful in corroborating the anti-obsessive claims. Another problem with clomipramine is the severe side effects which appear to affect a significant percentage of the patients taking this medication (S. M. Turner, Beidel, & Nathan, 1985).

The usefulness of any compound is diminished if a substantial percentage of the population cannot comfortably ingest the medication. Clomipramine can be administered intravenously, and this appears to eliminate some of the side effects (Warneke, 1984). However, this method of administration does not solve the problem of medication maintenance. As noted, discontinuation of the medication results in a return of symptoms. Therefore, it appears that maintenance doses are necessary, and, for the safety of the patient and ease of administration, this necessitates oral dosing.

If, as we believe at the present, the anti-obsessional effect of clomipramine or any other pharmacological agent is still open to empirical investigation, is there still a role for medication in the treatment of obsessive–compulsive disorder? We believe the answer to this question is a qualified yes. However, except for specific treatment protocols, the treatment plans developed for our patients never consist solely of medication. Yet, drugs often form an integral part of our overall intervention. Based on our own clinical experience, most obsessional patients are extremely distressed, and many meet the criteria for major depressive disorder. The data from Foa et al. (1983) indicate that these patients do not respond to behavioral interventions if a significant level of depression is evident.

Therefore, for patients who appear significantly depressed, it would seem prudent to administer a trial of antidepressant medication in an effort to improve their affective state prior to instituting behavior therapy. This is our standard course of action for patients with significant levels of depression.

Of the drugs available for clinical use in the United States, we do not believe that there currently is any empirical data available to strongly support the use of a specific drug, although we tend to favor those that have a higher serotonergic blockade action. We use a drug for its ability to improve the depressed mood state and find that the patients are much more willing and better able to tolerate the distress induced by the flooding sessions once their affect has improved. They also report less irritability and improved sleep. One patient reported to us that the medication (in this case, amitriptyline) does not help the obsessions or compulsions, but it does take the edge off her mood disturbance.

Another example of the utility of medication when combined with behavior therapy can be found in Mrs. C.'s description of her treatment in chapter 4. She appeared to us to be somewhat depressed when she began treatment, and we were unsure if medication would be of use to her. We, in conjunction with the patient, decided to initially conduct the treatment without medication. It quickly became apparent to us that her mood was such that she was unable to carry out the instructions completely. A trial of amitriptyline was instituted, and after several weeks, she reported an improved mood but no change in her primary symptoms. The behavior therapy program was restarted and as is evident from her report, was very successful.

SUMMARY

In this chapter we have discussed the use of pharmacological interventions in the treatment of obsessive–compulsive disorder. Our review of the literature indicates that although there are several promising medications available, the claims for an anti-obsessional effect have yet to be fully substantiated. There does appear to be some research evidence that medications with a serotonergic action or a combined serotonergic–noradrenergic action are the most effective. However, the improvement rates when medication is used alone indicate an average decrease in symptoms of 28 to 34%. This is rather low and indicates to us that the most effective strategy might be a combination of medication and behavior therapy. The use of medication might be particularly appropriate in alleviating the depressed mood of obsessionals so that they are more able to participate in a program of flooding and response prevention.

Chapter 7
Maintaining Treatment Gains

FOLLOW-UP STUDIES

One way to judge the effect of treatment interventions is to compare their outcome with the natural course of the disorder. As we noted in chapter 4, without treatment the clinical course of obsessive–compulsive disorder is usually chronic and unremitting, although in a minority of patients it appears to be of a more episodic nature, commonly characterized by periodic partial remissions. In a review of early studies, Goodwin, Guze, and Robins (1969) noted that the specific patient sample under study could be one variable affecting reports of the clinical course, with outpatient populations more likely to have discrete episodes and hospitalized patients likely to experience a more chronic course. They further reported that between 5% and 10% of patients show progressive deterioration. They concluded that the differences appeared to be directly related to the severity of the disorder, as the more dysfunctional patients are more likely to be hospitalized.

With respect to treated patients, recent studies of relapse and remission rates appear to indicate that approximately 70% to 80% of patients treated with behavioral methods maintained their treatment gains at 1-year follow-up (Kirk, 1983; Steketee et al., 1982). In this chapter, we will discuss the results of the various follow-up studies and what factors appear to exert significant influence in maintenance of treatment effects. The review will be limited to the study findings at follow-up and avoids extensive discussion of the results at posttreatment.

In a general survey of relapse rates for patients treated at a behavioral clinic, Kirk (1983) reviewed the files of 36 patients who had received behavioral interventions. Follow-up covered a period of between 1 and 5 years posttreatment, with an average of 3 years. The files were examined for further contacts with psychiatric clinics after the initial treatment period. In 81% of the cases, there was no evidence of further referral. Five cases had been referred back for further behavioral treatment, one had been treated with antidepressants and support, and one had been referred to another hospital. The author suggested that behavior therapy was an effective strategy for the many patients with obsessive–compulsive disorder. However, all of these cases were treated as outpatients, and this improvement rate might reflect only patients with a milder form of the disorder.

One of the first controlled studies specifically directed at assessing the long-term follow-up of behavioral treatment was published by Marks, Hodgson, and Rachman (1975). Twenty OCD patients were treated with in vivo exposure and self-imposed response prevention. Significant improvement in symptoms was found after exposure, and this improvement was still evident at the follow-up assessment conducted 2 years later. Improvement ratings consisted of patient rating scales and interviews with a subset of the patients and their relatives. Compared with baseline, at 2-year follow-up, 14 patients were rated as much improved, one as improved, and five as unchanged. Treatment gains were maintained in the areas of obsessions, attitude, depression, and general anxiety. Three of the successful cases did require booster sessions. There was a strong association between response to treatment during the first 3 weeks and outcome at 2-year follow-up. This association was even stronger when outcomes at 6-month follow-up and 2-year follow-up were compared. These data suggest that in many instances, the therapist is able to evaluate within a short period of time whether or not the treatment will be effective, and, when it is effective, gains are likely to be maintained. It also appears unlikely that those who show minimal response to treatment will undergo spontaneous remission during follow-up.

Foa and her colleagues (Foa, 1979; Foa et al., 1983; Steketee et al., 1982) have investigated the characteristics of those patients who do not respond to standard behavioral procedures. As we have noted in chapters 1, 2 and 4, these include patients who manifest overvalued ideation and severe depression. Foa (1979) reported that individuals with these characteristics do not respond to behavioral treatments based on an extinction model. Those with overvalued ideation habituate within sessions, but not between sessions, and those with severe depression do not show habituation either within or between sessions.

In a second article (Foa et al., 1983), there was an attempt to construct a model to predict success and failure in the behavioral treatment of obsessive–compulsive disorder. The variables included in a regression analysis consisted of demographic data, pretreatment symptomatology, and exposure-session responses. Pretreatment symptoms were assessed by self-ratings of severity of obsessions and compulsions, pretreatment depression and anxiety, and an independent assessor's rating of symptom severity. The measure during the exposure session was the patient's subjective anxiety rating, which was reported at the beginning of the session and at 10-minute intervals thereafter. Change in reported level of anxiety during the session was used as a measure of initial reactivity and habituation. At posttreatment, the patients were classified as *much improved* (improvement of 70% when compared with baseline); *improved* (improvement of 31% to 69%), and *failures* (improvement of 30% or less). At posttreatment, 58% were much improved, 38% improved, and 4% failed. At 2-year follow-up, 59% were much improved, 17% improved, and 24% failed. The regression model indicated that higher levels of pretreatment anxiety and depression, initial reactivity, within-session habituation, and between-session habituation were all significantly related to outcome at posttreatment. All of these variables, as well as age at symptom onset and posttreatment status, were significantly related to treatment maintenance. The results of these findings support the importance of Foa's (1979) earlier observations of a poor prognosis for those with overvalued ideation and untreated severe depression. The results further underscore the necessity to achieve both within-session and between-session habituation when using exposure treatments.

An interesting aspect of the Foa et al. (1983) study was the shift in the number of patients classified as *improved* or *failures* from posttreatment to follow-up. Correlations between posttreatment outcome and follow-up indicated that those who were significantly improved at posttreatment maintained their treatment gains, and those who were failures did not show spontaneous improvement. The group that showed partial improvement (*improved*) were equally as likely to maintain their gains as to relapse. Thus, partial improvement represents a tenuous condition, one that, although possibly unavoidable in a research protocol, should probably not be accepted in routine clinical practice. Partial improvement suggests that the treatment is probably effective and that continued treatment sessions might result in further consolidation of gains. Finally, the results of this study highlighted the importance of an active maintenance program where signs of relapse can be detected early and booster sessions quickly implemented.

Specific cognitive styles have also been indirectly related to maintaining treatment gains (R. M. Turner, Newman, & Foa, 1983). It had been previously suggested that patients with OCD manifested an overinclusive style (Foa & Steketee, 1979). To examine this contention, the Neufeld Task was administered to a group of 12 OCD patients. This task requires the subject to rate the similarity of meanings of two emotional adjectives. Individuals without a psychiatric diagnosis utilize three conceptual dimensions when rating the adjectives. However, schizophrenics use four dimensions, suggesting they have an overinclusive style.

In this study, the majority of the OCD patients (75%) utilized only one dimension when making similarity ratings, indicating an underinclusive rather than overinclusive style. Such a cognitive style has been referred to as *stereotypic obsessiveness*. A small subset (25%) manifested a "normal" cognitive style, using three dimensions to construct their similarity ratings. All patients were treated for their obsessive–compulsive disorder using standard behavioral procedures, and both groups were equally improved at posttreatment. However, at a 1-year follow-up assessment, there were significant differences in maintenance of treatment effects. The patients in the normal inclusive group chose to terminate therapy at posttreatment but were observed to have relapsed after 1 year. Those who were in the underinclusive group, even though they had made identical improvements, chose to continue therapy throughout the follow-up period and, at the assessment, had maintained their treatment gains. The small sample size precludes much generalization, but it could be that the stereotypic obsessiveness of this second group of patients was important in maintaining treatment gains. Their all-or-nothing cognitive style might have kept them from accepting "partial" improvement, and through continuing therapeutic contact, served to prevent relapse during the follow-up period.

In one of the few long-term follow-up studies using both pharmacological and behavioral interventions, 37 chronic OCD patients were assessed for maintenance of treatment effects (Mawson et al., 1982). The treatment regimen consisted of a 36-week drug trial with randomization to either clomipramine or placebo treatment. In addition, half of the subjects in each experimental condition received 15 hours of exposure in vivo, and the other half received 30 hours. At 2-year follow-up, all treatment gains had been maintained or showed further improvement, and the initial superiority of the clomipramine group had disappeared for all variables but measures of leisure time and social relationships. There were no differences between the drug groups for any ritual or mood variables, with all groups manifesting substantial clinical gains. More exposure sessions (30 rather than 15 hours) predicted more improvement of rituals at 2-year follow-up but did not predict mood or social adjustment.

In a recent effort to address more specifically factors involved in relapse, Espie (1986) constructed a group-treatment program for OCD patients who had responded originally to behavioral treatment but had relapsed an average of 8 months later. The group program consisted of 10 weekly meetings specifically designed to reduce OCD symptoms and also to prevent future relapse. Thus, in addition to "booster" sessions of in vivo exposure, response prevention, and homework assignments, anti-relapse elements were included. These components included spouse involvement to maintain adequate levels of reinforcement for refraining from ritualization, future planning of life goals (possibly to expand socialization networks and fill leisure time previously consumed by ritualization), and discrimination training to identify early signs of relapse such as irrational thinking and compulsive behavior. This program was effective in bringing active symptomatology into remission and maintaining treatment gains at the 1-year follow-up period. Again, the small sample size precludes drawing general conclusions, but if the study can be replicated, it would appear that specific attention to factors previously associated with relapse can in fact assist in the prevention of future episodes.

ISSUES IN MAINTAINING TREATMENT GAINS

In general, relatively little attention has been paid to issues of follow-up and relapse prevention in the treatment of obsessive–compulsive disorder. The reasons for this are unclear, but as noted by S. M. Turner and Michelson (1984), until recently the outlook for improvement with treatment was dismal. Without effective treatments, relapse prevention could have been a moot point. However, the incorporation of behavioral strategies and new drug compounds has vastly improved the rate of successful treatment outcome. Therefore, researchers and clinicians must begin to address the issue of maintaining treatment gains.

The importance of the need for an active maintenance program has been noted by several investigators. For example, in the study by Foa et al. (1983), those who were rated *improved* were as likely to relapse as to make further improvements. Although it is unclear exactly what is meant by these ratings, it is clear that, particularly for those patients who report partial symptom remission, the immediate posttreatment period is a crucial time.

The importance of follow-up can also be demonstrated from data in the study by R. M. Turner et al. (1983). Patients who remained in therapy during the follow-up year maintained their treatment gains whereas those who chose to discontinue therapeutic contact during follow-up relapsed. R. M. Turner et al. calculated the cost of follow-up therapy and concluded that treatment without follow-up, although cost-efficient, could not be judged effective over a longer time period.

Among the variables viewed as crucial to treatment maintenance are home treatment sessions (especially when active treatment has been conducted on an inpatient unit) and family involvement (Marks et al., 1975). Espie (1986) has also noted the significance of spousal involvement to maintain adequate reinforcement during follow-up. In addition, future planning of life goals and patient training to identify early signs of relapse were targeted as important areas of relapse prevention. Although viewed as necessary, familial involvement in maintaining gains cannot be unilaterally recommended. As noted in the treatment chapter, a careful evaluation of the strength of the marital and familial relationships must be completed before considering their inclusion in a maintenance program.

In addition to the research findings, there are clinical reasons for instituting an active maintenance program. Following an aggressive (and usually time-limited) intervention, there is a need for a consolidation of treatment gains. We believe that gains are best maintained by close and careful monitoring of the patient for a period of 1 or 2 years after active intervention. As we have noted throughout this volume, obsessive–compulsive disorder is a chronic condition. Although many patients can be helped by behavior therapy, pharmacotherapy, or some combination of these two interventions, it is likely that most patients will experience some vestige of the disorder for their entire lives. This can include increased nervousness, rigidity of cognitive styles or activity schedules, and an occasional intrusive thought, which, unlike prior to treatment, no longer remains with the patient. Furthermore, even with structured follow-up, it is likely that some percentage of patients (possibly under periods of stress) will experience a return of the full-blown syndrome. Without continued treatment maintenance, return of the primary symptoms is virtually assured.

There are many clinical issues that dictate the necessity for continued therapist–patient contact long after the primary intervention sessions have been completed. These considerations can be grouped into three categories: primary symptoms, secondary symptoms, and interpersonal functioning. With respect to the first category, the most obvious example is when a patient is treated on an inpatient unit. Many fears of OCD patients are not situationally bound, that is, contamination by germs occurs no matter where the patient might be. However, in a substantial number of cases, patients report that their symptoms are most intense in their homes. We have seen several patients whose symptoms remitted after hospital treatment, only to reappear in full force upon discharge and return home. Thus, even when the patient has demonstrated significant improvement in the hospital setting, continued intervention in the form of home visits will be necessary. Particularly for those whose rituals are centered around the home, we believe that at least two treatment sessions conducted in the home are necessary for the transfer of treatment gains. We hasten to add that these visits are not home monitoring visits but actual flooding and response-prevention sessions carried out in the patient's home.

As we noted earlier, an intensive intervention strategy can result in a dramatic change in the primary symptomatology. Other cognitive changes require more time, and many patients report that they are unable to believe fully that "nothing is going to happen." As one of our patients phrased it "I still feel like I am waiting for the other shoe to drop." These patients, although markedly improved, are still in a tenuous emotional state, maintaining a chronic residual anxiety state. While they are in this state, it is possible that events related to the obsessive thoughts will actually occur. Some examples include physical illnesses of the patient that might result in hospitalization or the death of a relative from cancer. Although the cancer was not "caused" by contamination, the catastrophic event nonetheless occurs at a point where the patient feared something would happen. In a perfect world, these events would occur only after a treatment-consolidation period. However, these events cannot be controlled, and without an established plan of treatment maintenance, their introduction immediately after treatment could result in patient relapse.

An example might help to illustrate this point more clearly. A patient with a fear of cancer had been treated with a course of flooding and response prevention that had successfully eliminated the rituals and dramatically reduced the obsessional thinking. Normally, an uneventful maintenance period would result in further consolidation of these gains. However, soon after the end of treatment, the patient's mother died from cancer. This event mirrored the patient's obsessional thoughts, thus putting the patient at high probability for relapse. The presence of a structured maintenance program that includes frequent therapeutic visits would be effective in helping the patient deal with this event in the most positive fashion possible. No time would be wasted in reinstituting any active interventions to deal with the possible intensification of symptoms. For those without ongoing programs, gains could be lost before therapeutic contact was reinstituted. In actuality, whether or not these events occur, continued contact during the first year will always allow for early detection of relapse and immediate reinstitution of therapeutic strategies.

Other patient variables also dictate the need for active maintenance programs. For example, patients need to learn how to control their residual general anxiety and could benefit from anxiety-management techniques. In other instances, we have found that some patients with obsessive–compulsive disorder also have many interpersonal difficulties. The deficiencies might be in basic social skills or general assertiveness. The relationship between social skills deficits and anxiety has been well documented (cf., Hersen & Bellack, 1976). The inability to function effectively in interpersonal interactions could lead to increased anxiety and perhaps a return of the symptoms. One patient expressed such a train of events thus: "When I feel someone is taking advantage of me and I do not respond appropriately, I begin to feel very anxious. Then I start feeling the urge to retrace my steps and check." The maintenance phase is the ideal time to address additional problem areas. Specific procedures used to deal with secondary symptoms will be discussed later.

Finally, as we have noted several times, the severity of obsessive–compulsive disorder exerts an impact upon all aspects of social functioning. Many patients have given up life roles as spouse, parent, or breadwinner. Improvement in the patient does not automatically result in an improved marital relationship, and marital or family therapy could be indicated. In addition, with symptom remission, there are expectations that the patient will reassume these responsibilities. During the maintenance period, the therapist can assist the patient in the gradual re-acquisition of these roles. Most patients also need assistance in finding new activities through which to fill the time previously allocated to perfoming the rituals. It has been our clinical experience, and that of Espie (1986), that those patients who do not find alternative activities are more likely to relapse.

PRACTICAL STRATEGIES FOR MAINTAINING TREATMENT GAINS

Maintenance Timetable

For some patients, simply maintaining regular appointments with the therapist serves as an effective maintenance strategy. Just keeping in touch provides an extra check on controlling the rituals and seems to reassure the patient. As expressed by one patient, "Coming here is like going to confession. Knowing that I have to tell you what I did, right or wrong, makes me try all the harder." Although for some patients, checking in might be all that is necessary, the therapist must still decide upon the frequency of the sessions.

Similarly, the therapist should determine when a sufficient number of visits has been made and guard against overdependency. We have found that a gradual decrease in the number of meetings is quite effective. Once the active intervention has been completed, we continue to meet with the patient 2 or 3 times per week for at least 2 to 4 weeks. Each of these sessions can be quite short (30 or 40 minutes), but it does provide ample opportunity for troubleshooting any new problem situations that might arise and evaluating the patient's response in these new situations. The schedule is then readjusted to once or twice per week. During this time, each session can be of a longer duration (60 minutes).

In addition to providing support, it is during this phase that other active interventions that might be necessary should be introduced. If these are necessary, then the new interventions dictate the length and number of sessions. If other problems are not addressed, the once- or twice-a-week meetings can be used to assist the patient in the resumption of life roles and the expansion of a social network. Many patients, having been isolated for so long, need specific instructions or training in how to begin this resocialization process. Contingency contracts and homework assignments can be useful in getting the patient started.

If there are no signs of relapse, the maintenance sessions should be scaled back to weekly, biweekly, bimonthly, monthly meetings or any other schedule that appears appropriate for a particular patient. The final discharge decision must be made jointly by therapist and patient and should be based on the patient's overall clinical status.

Transfer of Therapeutic Responsibility

If therapy is to be successful, responsibility for its effectiveness will have to be transferred from the therapist to the patient. Initially, the therapist assumed primary control for conducting therapy. Recall that we discussed problems associated with allowing patients to determine treatment strategy. Gradually, as the patient's condition improves, he or she realizes that self-control can be exerted over the behaviors. In addition, the patient learns that avoidance of feared situations or rituals function to increase the fear, whereas extended or frequent contact that is not followed by ritualization eliminates the anxiety. This understanding is a necessary part of the transfer of responsibility and usually occurs toward the end of active treatment. Sometime the patient uses this understanding and actively assumes treatment responsibility. That is, he or she independently initiates exposure to the stimulus that is feared. In other instances, the patient is less likely to seek out further exposure situations. In these cases, the therapist has to use a more structured approach, based on Socratic dialogue and problem-solving training to prompt the patient to assume this active role.

Introduction of Additional Treatment Interventions

As noted, patients rarely present with *just* obsessive–compulsive disorder. Rather, there are often a myriad of problems, some of which might be a direct result of the primary disorder and others which might be independent in etiology but still play a role in maintenance of treatment gains. An example of the first category might be a strained marital relationship, which does not necessarily disappear with the remission of the primary symptoms. Difficulties in the second category include unassertiveness and generalized anxiety. In these cases, the relationship between the primary disorder and the secondary difficulties is less clear. However, stress and stressful life events do appear to play a role in the onset and exacerbation of the primary OCD symptoms, and it is likely that factors such as poor interpersonal skill increase anxiety and exacerbate symptoms. We noted an example of how this might work in an earlier section of this chapter. In fact, for clinical purposes, the specific etiology is probably unimportant. What is important is that if left untreated, these secondary problems could figure prominently in relapse. Thus, it is necessary to address these symptoms during the maintenance phase.

Most of the therapeutic strategies can probably be conceptualized as some form of anxiety-management procedure. It is important to note here that we consider these procedures *supplemental* treatment. They have not been found to be effective in the treatment of primary OCD symptoms and should not be considered substitutes for flooding and response prevention. In fact, it has been our experience that none of these supplemental strategies is very useful until the primary symptoms are under control. One example of a supplemental strategy is relaxation training. Although typically not effective in decreasing anxiety related to obsessions and compulsions, it can be an effective intervention for the remitted patient who still complains of some feelings of general anxiety. Similarly, social-skills training could be effective in improving interpersonal relations, which can lead to more satisfying and therefore less anxiety-producing interactions. Marital or family therapy might also be indicated to assist in the readjustment to life roles and to improve strained relationships. In general, any intervention that would serve to decrease life stress could improve the probability of maintaining treatment gains.

Therapists are cautioned against becoming overly optimistic in their expectations of a full remission. It is likely that most patients will experience at least one relapse. However, patients can be educated about early warning signs of relapse and the importance of self-exposure should symptoms begin to recur. This self-recognition, coupled with encouragement to return to the clinic for booster sessions can assist in preventing the occurrence of the full disorder.

REFLECTION BY MRS. C. 1 YEAR POSTTREATMENT

Once I had been through the treatment program at Western Psychiatric Institute and Clinic, I was able to use what I had learned during my previous years of psychotherapy, especially the relaxation training and thought-stopping. On some occasions prior to treatment with Dr. Turner, I had been successful with these procedures, but it took a therapist working with me in my home to release me completely from the grip of my compulsion and allow me to actually feel it lift and leave me. There have been a few times during this past year when the urges have come back momentarily, but they were never as intense and never strong enough for me to give in to them. Just a little distraction, relaxation, or thought-stopping has helped me to dismiss the thoughts and feelings and control my behavior. I never again want to get into the situation I was in prior to entering therapy.

My life has changed in many ways since I received treatment. The main difference is that I do not live with the heavy weight of having to constantly be on guard against any possibility of contamination by animals or people who have pets. Several times during the past year I would forget for a split second and tense at a chipmunk running across our yard or my child reaching out to pet a puppy. Then I would suddenly realize that I no longer needed to carry out the rituals. I would feel the pressure lifting and evaporating. It was such a good feeling.

This difference is the reason for all the other changes in my life and the lives of everyone in my family. The children can have their friends inside to play anytime. It is fun to watch my son with seven boys crowded around the computer and my daughter with three other girls playing dress up in her room. My husband can have his family come to visit at any time. We can visit a home with a pet and not have to change clothes or wash when we come home. I am no longer afraid to get close to people for fear that they might want to visit me in my home.

The rituals I engaged in must have consumed more of my time than I had ever realized. I know I remember thinking that washing one more thing would not take very long, but it all eventually became endless. I am doing things now that I never thought I would have enough time for while caring for a family. When I finally settled into a normal daily routine after treatment, I decided to return to nursing. I had not worked outside the home for almost 11 years, so this was a big adjustment for everyone in the family. I accepted an on-call position at a long-term health care facility. I work there about two shifts a week. This leaves me the opportunity to still attend my son's basketball games, be homeroom mother at school, accompany my daughter's class on field trips, drive her to dance class and Brownies, and attend church activities such as my younger daughter's preschool program. I also decided to continue my education and enrolled in the nursing degree program at our local university. I have taken two courses since concluding treatment and plan to pursue this full-time after my youngest child enters school.

A very visible change in my life is that our house and car are never as clean as they were 1 year ago. However, my life is more productive. My view of myself has changed in that I have come to better accept myself for what I am. I realize that it is all right not to be the perfect wife, mother, nurse, or student. Much more can be accomplished when attention to detail is not carried to extremes. Much more can also be accomplished in the absence of the stress of trying to be perfect. My view of others has changed in one specific way. I no longer characterize people according to those who have pets and those who do not.

SUMMARY

In this chapter we have briefly discussed the follow-up data on treatment of obsessive–compulsive disorder. Although many patients, particularly those treated with behavioral methods, appear to maintain their treatment gains, there are a significant number who do relapse. An examination of the research data, as well as our own clinical experience, points out the importance of the inclusion of specific strategies to aid maintenance and the need for an active maintenance program. We think the comments of our patient Mrs. C. are illustrative of the experience of many patients following active treatment. In particular, we want to draw the reader's attention to the continual unfolding of newly discovered abilities and desires once the patient became free of the primary symptoms.

References

Akhtar, S., Wig, N. H., Verna, V. K., Pershod, D., & Verna, S. K. (1975). A phenomenological analysis of symptoms in obsessive–compulsive neuroses. *British Journal of Psychiatry, 127,* 342–348.

Allen, J. J., & Tune, G. S. (1975). The Lynfield Obsessional/Compulsive Questionnaire. *Scottish Medical Journal, 20,* 21–24.

American Psychiatric Association (1987). *Diagnostic and statistical manual of mental disorders.* (3rd ed.—rev.) Washington, DC: American Psychiatric Association.

Ananth, J. (1976). Treatment of obsessive-compulsive neurosis: Pharmacological approach. *Psychosomatics, 17,* 180–184.

Ananth, J. (1983). Clomipramine in obsessive–compulsive disorder: A review. *Psychosomatics, 24,* 723–727.

Ananth, J. (1985). Clomipramine in obsessive neurosis: A review. In M. Mavissakalian, S. M. Turner, & L. Michelson (Eds.), *Obsessive-compulsive disorder: psychological and pharmacological treatment.* (pp. 167–211). New York: Plenum.

Ananth, J. (1986). Clomipramine: An antiobsessive drug. *Canadian Journal of Psychiatry, 31,* 253–258.

Ananth, J., Pecknold, J., Van Den Steen, N., & Engelsmann, F. (1981). Double-blind comparative study of clomipramine and amitriptyline in obsessive neurosis. *Progress in Neuro-Psychopharmacology and Biological Psychiatry, 5,* 257–262.

Asberg, M., Thoren, P., & Bertilsson, L. (1982). Clomipramine treatment of obsessive-disorder. Biochemical and clinical aspects. *Psychopharmacology Bulletin, 18,* 13–21.

Barlow, D. H. (1985). The dimensions of anxiety disorders. In A. H. Tuma & J. D. Maser (Eds.), *Anxiety and the anxiety disorders* (pp. 479–500). Hillsdale, NJ: Lawrence Erlbaum.

Baum, M. (1970). Extinction of avoidance responding through response prevention (flooding). *Psychological Bulletin, 74,* 276–284.

Baxter, L. R. (1985). Two cases of obsessive–compulsive disorder with depression responsive to trazodone. *Journal of Nervous and Mental Disease, 173,* 432–433.

Beck, A. T. (1976). *Cognitive therapy and emotional disorders.* New York: International Universities Press.

Beck, A. T., & Emery, G. (1985). *Anxiety disorders and phobias: A cognitive perspective.* New York: Basic Books.

Beech, H. R., Ciesielski, K. T., & Gordon, P. K. (1983). Further observations of evoked potentials in obsessional patients. *British Journal of Psychiatry, 142,* 605–609.

Beech, H. R., & Vaughan, M. (1978). *Behavioral treatment of obsessional states.* New York: John Wiley & Sons.

Beidel, D. C., & Turner, S. M. (1986). A critique of the theoretical bases of cognitive-behavioral theories and therapy. *Clinical Psychology Review, 6,* 177–197.

Beidel, D. C., Turner, S. M., & Allgood-Hill, B. (1986, November). The use of videotape exposure sessions in the treatment of obsessive–compulsive disorder. Paper presented at the meeting of the Association for Advancement of Behavior Therapy Annual Convention, Chicago.

Black, A. (1974). The natural history of obsessional neurosis. In H. R. Beech (Ed.), *Obsessional states* (pp. 19–54). London: Methuen.

Boulougouris, J., & Bassiakos, L. (1973). Prolonged flooding in cases with obsessive-compulsive neurosis. *Behaviour Research and Therapy, 11,* 227–231.

Boyd, J. H., Burke, J. D., Gruenberg, E., Holzer, C. E. III, Rae, D. S., George, L. K., Karno, M., Stolzman, R., McEvoy, L., & Nestadt, G. (1984). Exclusion criteria of DSM-III: A study of co-occurrence of hierarchy-free syndromes. *Archives of General Psychiatry, 41,* 983–989.

Carroll, B. J., Feinberg, M., Greden, J. F., Toriska, J., Albala, A. A., Kronfal, Z., Lohr, N., Steiner, M., de Vigne, J. P., & Young, E. (1981). A specific laboratory test for the diagnosis of melancholia: Standardization, validation and clinical utility. *Archives of General Psychiatry, 38,* 15–22.

Ciesielski, K. T., Beech, H. R., & Gordon, P. K. (1981). Some electrophysiological observations in obsessional states. *British Journal of Psychiatry, 138,* 479–484.

Cooper, J. E. (1970). The Leyton Obsessional Inventory. *Psychological Medicine, 1,* 48–64.

Cooper, J., & Kelleher, M. (1973). The Leyton Obsessional Inventory: A principal components analysis on normal subjects. *Psychological Medicine, 3,* 204–208.

Coryell, W. (1981). Obsessive–compulsive disorder and primary unipolar depression: Comparisons of background, family history, course and mortality. *Journal of Nervous and Mental Disease, 169,* 220–224.

Cottraux, J. A., Bouvard, M., Claustrat, B., & Juenet, C. (1984). Abnormal dexamethasone suppression test in primary obsessive–compulsive patients: A confirmatory report. *Psychiatry Research, 13,* 157–165.

Crighel, E., & Solomonovici, A. (1968). Electroclinical correlations in neurosis with anxiety and depression. *Psychiatrica Clinica, 1,* 143–151.

Emmelkamp, P. M. G., & de Lange, I. (1983). Spouse involvement in the treatment of obsessive–compulsive patients. *Behaviour Research and Therapy, 21,* 341–346.

Emmelkamp, P. M. G., & Kraanen, J. (1977). Therapist-controlled exposure *in vivo* versus self-controlled exposure *in vivo*: A comparison with obsessive–compulsive patients. *Behaviour Research and Therapy, 15,* 491–495.

Emmelkamp, P. M. G., & Kwee, K. G. (1977). Obsessional ruminations: A comparison between thought-stopping and prolonged exposure in imagination. *Behaviour Research and Therapy, 15,* 441–444.

Epstein, A. W., & Bailine, S. H. (1971). Sleep and dream studies in obsessional neurosis with particular reference to epileptic states. *Biological Psychiatry, 3,* 149–158.

Espie, C. A. (1986). The group treatment of obsessive–compulsive ritualizers: Behavioural management of identified patterns of relapse. *Behavioural Psychotherapy, 14,* 21–33.

Flament, M. F., Rapoport, J. L., Berg, C. J., Scaeery, W., Kilts, C., Mellstrom, B., & Lennoila, M. (1985). Clomipramine treatment of childhood obsessive–compulsive disorder: A double-blind controlled study. *Archives of General Psychiatry, 42,* 977–983.

Flor-Henry, P., Yeudall, L. T., Koles, Z. J., & Howarth, B. G. (1979). Neuropsychological and power spectral EEG investigations of the obsessive–compulsive syndrome. *Biological Psychiatry, 14,* 119–130.

Foa, E. B. (1979). Failure in treating obsessive–compulsives. *Behaviour Research and Therapy, 17,* 169–176,

Foa, E. B., Grayson, J. B., Steketee, G. S., Doppelt, H. G., Turner, R. M., & Latimer, P. R. (1983). Success and failure in the behavioral treatment of obsessive–compulsives. *Journal of Consulting and Clinical Psychology, 51,* 287–297.

Foa, E. B., & Steketee, G. (1979). Obsessive–compulsives: Conceptual issues and treatment interventions. In M. Hersen, R. M., Eisler, & P. M. Miller (Eds.), *Progress in behavior modification*. Vol. 8. (pp. 1–53). New York: Academic Press.

Foa, E. B., Steketee, G., & Grayson, J. B. (1985). Imaginal and in vivo exposure: A comparison with obsessive–compulsive checkers. *Behavior Therapy, 16,* 292–302.

Foa, E. B., Steketee, G. S., & Ozarow, B. J. (1985). Behavior therapy with obsessive–compulsives: From theory to treatment. In M. Mavissakalian, S. M. Turner, & L. Michelson (Eds.), *Obsessive–compulsive disorder: Psychological and pharmacological treatment* (pp. 49–129). New York: Plenum.

Foa, E. B., Steketee, G., Turner, R. M., & Fischer, S. C. (1980). Effects of imaginal exposure to feared disasters in obsessive–compulsive checkers. *Behaviour Research and Therapy, 18,* 449–455.

Fontaine, R., & Chouinard, G. (1986). An open clinical trial of fluoxetine in the treatment of obsessive–compulsive disorder. *Journal of Clinical Psychopharmacology, 6,* 98–101.

Foulds, G. A. (1965). *Personality and personal illness.* London: Tavistock.

Foulds, G. A., & Caine, T. M. (1958). Psychoneurotic symptom clusters, trail clusters, and psychological tests. *Journal of Mental Science, 104,* 722.

Foulds, G. A., & Caine, T. M. (1959). Symptom clusters and personality types among psychoneurotic men compared with women. *Journal of Mental Science, 105,* 469.

Goodwin, D. W., Guze, S. B., & Robins, E. (1969). Follow-up studies in obsessional neurosis. *Archives of General Psychiatry, 20,* 182–187.

Grayson, J. B., Foa, E. B., & Steketee, G. (1982). Habituation during exposure treatment: Distraction vs. attention focusing. *Behaviour Research and Therapy, 20,* 323–328.

Grayson, J. B., Foa, E. B., & Steketee, G. (1986). Exposure in vivo of obsessive–compulsives under distracting and attention-focusing conditions: Replication and extension. *Behaviour Research and Therapy, 24,* 475–479.

Grimshaw, L. (1965). The outcome of obsessional disorder: A follow-up study of 100 cases. *British Journal of Psychiatry, 111,* 1051–1056.

Hare, E., Price, J., & Slater, E. (1971). Age distribution of schizophrenia and neurosis: Findings in a national sample. *British Journal of Psychiatry, 119,* 445–458.

Hersen, M., & Bellack, A. S. (1976). Social skills training for chronic psychiatric patients: Rationale, research findings, and future directions. *Comprehensive Psychiatry, 17,* 559–580.

Hodgson, R., & Rachman, S. (1972). The effects of contamination and washing in obsessional patients. *Behaviour Research and Therapy, 10,* 111–117.

Hodgson, R. J., & Rachman, S. (1977). Obsessional–compulsive complaints. *Behaviour Research and Therapy, 15,* 389–395.

Hodgson, R. J., Rachman, S., & Marks, I. M. (1972). The treatment of chronic obsessive–compulsive neurosis: Follow-up and further findings. *Behaviour Research and Therapy, 10,* 181–189.

Hornsveld, R. H. J., Kraaimaat, F. W., & van Dam-Baggen, R. M. J. (1979). Anxiety/discomfort and handwashing in obsessive–compulsive and psychiatric control patients. *Behaviour Research and Therapy, 17,* 223–228.

Ingram, I. M. (1961). Obsessional illness in mental hospital patients. *Journal of Mental Science, 197,* 382–402.

Insel, T. R., & Akiskal, H. S. (1986). Obsessive-compulsive disorder with psychotic features: A phenomenologic analysis. *American Journal of Psychiatry, 143,* 530–532.

Insel, T. R., Donnelly, E. F., Lalakea, M. L., Alterman, I. S., & Murphy, D. L. (1983). Neurological and neuropsychological studies of patients with obsessive–compulsive disorder. *Biological Psychiatry, 18,* 741–751.

Insel, T. R., Gillin, C., Moore, A., Mendelson, W. B., Loewenstein, R. J., & Murphy, D. L. (1982). The sleep of patients with obsessive-compulsive disorder. *Archives of General Psychiatry, 39,* 1372–1377.

Insel, T. R., Kalin, N. H., Guttmacher, L. B., Cohen, R. M., & Murphy, D. L. (1982). The dexamethasone suppression test in patients with primary obsessive–compulsive disorder. *Psychiatry Research, 6,* 153–160.

Insel, T. R., Mueller, E. A., Alterman, I., Linnoila, M., & Murphy, D. L. (1985). Obsessive–compulsive disorder and serotonin: Is there a connection? *Biological Psychiatry, 20,* 1174–1188.

Insel, T. R., Mueller, E. A., Gillin, C., Siever, L. J., & Murphy, D. L. (1985). Tricyclic response in obsessive–compulsive disorder. *Progress in Neuro-Psychopharmacology and Biological Psychiatry, 9,* 25–31.

Jacob, R. G., Ford, R. R., & Turner, S. M. (1985). Obsessive–compulsive disorder. In M. Hersen (Ed.), *Practice of inpatient behavior therapy: A clinical guide* (pp. 61–91). Orlando, FL: Grune & Stratton.

Jaspers, K. (1963). *General psychopathology.* Chicago: University of Chicago.

Jenike, M. A., Baer, L., Minichiello, W. E., Schwartz, C. E., & Carey, R. J. Jr. (1986). Coexistent obsessive–compulsive disorder and schizotypal personality disorder: A poor prognostic indicator. *Archives of General Psychiatry, 43,* 296.

Jenike, M. A., & Brotman, A. W. (1984). The EEG in obsessive–compulsive disorder. *Journal of Clinical Psychiatry, 45,* 122–124.

Kahn, R. S., Westenberg, H. G. M., & Jolles, J. (1984). Zimelidine treatment of obsessive–compulsive disorder. *Acta Psychiatria Scandinavia, 69,* 259–261.

Kelly, D. (1973). Therapeutic outcome in limbic leucotomy in psychiatric patients. *Psychiatria Neurologia, and Neurochirugia, 76,* 353–363.

Kendler, K. S., Heath, A. C., Martin, N. G., & Eaves, L. J. (1987). Symptoms of anxiety and symptoms of depression: Same genes, different environments. *Archives of General Psychiatry, 44,* 451–457.

Kirk, J. W. (1983). Behavioural treatment of obsessive–compulsive patients in clinical practice. *Behaviour Research and Therapy, 21,* 57–62.

Kringlen, E. (1965). Obsessional neurotics: A long term follow-up. *British Journal of Psychiatry, 111,* 709–722.

Lang, P. J. (1977). Physiological assessment of anxiety and fear. In J. D. Cone & R. P. Hawkins (Eds.), *Behavioral assessment: New directions in clinical psychology* (pp. 178–195). New York: Brunner/Mazel.

Lang, P. J., Kozak, M. H., Miller, G. A., Levin, D. N., & McLean, A. (1980). Emotional imagery: Conceptual structure and pattern of somato-visceral response. *Psychophysiology, 17,* 179–192.

Lang, P. J., Levin, D. N., Miller, G. A., & Kozak, M. J. (1983). Fear behavior, fear imagery, and the psychophysiology of emotion: The problem of affective response integration. *Journal of Abnormal Psychology, 92,* 276–306.

Lieberman, J. A., Kane, J. M., Sarantakos, S., Cole, K., Howard, A., Borenstein, M., Novacenko, H., & Puig-Antich, J. (1985). Dexamethasone suppression tests in patients with obsessive–compulsive disorder. *American Journal of Psychiatry, 142,* 747–751.

Lo, W. (1967). A follow-up study of obsessional neurotics in Hong Kong Chinese. *British Journal of Psychiatry, 113,* 823–832.

Marks, I. (1985). Behavioral psychotherapy for anxiety disorders. *Psychiatric Clinics of North America, 8,* 25–35.

Marks, I. M., Hodgson, R., & Rachman, S. (1975). Treatment of chronic obsessive–compulsive neurosis by *in vivo* exposure: Two year follow-up and issues in treatment. *British Journal of Psychiatry, 127,* 349–364.

Marks, I. M., Stern, R. S., Mawson, D., Cobb, J., & McDonald, R. (1980). Clomipramine and exposure for obsessive–compulsive rituals. *British Journal of Psychiatry, 136,* 1–25.

Mavissakalian, M., & Hammen, M. S. (1986). DSM-III personality disorders and agoraphobia: II. Changes with treatment. *Comprehensive Psychiatry, 28,* 356–361.

Mavissakalian, M., Turner, S. M., Michelson, L., & Jacob, R. G. (1985). Tricyclic antidepressants in obsessive–compulsive disorder: II. Antiobsessional or antidepressant agents? *American Journal of Psychiatry, 142,* 572–576.

Mawson, D., Marks, I. M., & Ramm, L. (1982). Clomipramine and exposure for chronic obsessive–compulsive rituals: III. Two year follow-up and further findings. *British Journal of Psychiatry, 140,* 11–18.

McKeon, J., McGuffin, P., & Robinson, P. (1984). Obsessive-compulsive neurosis following head injury: A report of four cases. *British Journal of Psychiatry, 144,* 190–192.

Meyer, V. (1966). Modification of expectations in cases with obsessional rituals. *Behaviour Research and Therapy, 4,* 273–280.

Mischel, W. (1972). Direct vs. indirect personality assessment: Evidence and implications. *Journal of Consulting and Clinical Psychology, 38,* 319–324.

Montgomery, S. A. (1980). Clomipramine in obsessional neurosis: A placebo controlled trial. *Pharmacology and Medicine, 1,* 189–192.

Mullen, P. E., Linsell, C. R., & Parker, D. (1986). Influence of sleep disruption and caloric restriction on biological markers for depression. *Lancet, 2,* (8515) 1051–1055.

Munro, A. (1980). Monosymptomatic hypochondriacal psychosis (MHP): New aspects of an old syndrome. *Journal of Psychiatric Treatment and Evaluation, 2,* 79–86.

Pauls, D. L., Towbin, K. E., Leckman, J. F., Zahner, G. E. P., & Cohen, D. J. (1986). Gilles de la Tourette's Syndrome and obsessive–compulsive disorder. *Archives of General Psychiatry, 43,* 1180–1182.

Philpott, R. (1975). Recent advances in the behavioral measurement of obsessional illness: Difficulties common to these and other measures. *Scottish Medical Journal, 20,* 33–40.

Pollitt, J. (1957). Natural history of obsessional states. *British Medical Journal, 1,* 195–198.

Prasad, A. (1984). A double blind study of imipramine versus zimelidine in treatment of obsessive–compulsive neurosis. *Pharmacopsychiatry, 17,* 61–62.

Prasad, A. (1986). Efficacy of trazodone as an anti-obsessional agent. *Neuropsychobiology, 15,* 19–21.

Rabavilas, A., & Boulougouris, J. (1974). Physiological accompaniments of ruminations, flooding and thought-stopping in obsessive patients. *Behaviour Research and Therapy, 12,* 239–244.

Rachman, S. (1974). Primary obsessional slowness. *Behaviour Research and Therapy, 12,* 9–18.

Rachman, S. (1976). Obsessional-compulsive checking. *Behaviour Research and Therapy, 14,* 269–277.

Rachman, S. J. (1985). An overview of clinical and research issues in obsessive–compulsive disorders. In M. Mavissakalian, S. M. Turner, & L. Michelson (Eds.), *Obsessive–compulsive disorder: Psychological and pharmacological treatment* (pp. 1–47). New York: Plenum.

Rachman, S. J., & Hodgson, R. J. (1980). *Obsessions and compulsions.* Englewood Cliffs, NJ: Prentice-Hall.

Rachman, S., Marks, I., & Hodgson, R. (1973). The treatment of chronic obsessive–compulsive neurosis by modeling and flooding in vivo. *Behaviour Research and Therapy, 11,* 467–471.

Rapoport, J. L. (1986). Childhood obsessive–compulsive disorder. *Journal of Child Psychology and Psychiatry, 27,* 289–295.

Rasmussen, S. A. (1984). Lithium and tryptophan augmentation in clomipramine-resistant obsessive–compulsive disorder. *American Journal of Psychiatry, 141,* 1283–1285.

Rasmussen, S. A., & Tsuang, M. T. (1986). Clinical characteristics and family history in DSM-III obsessive–compulsive disorder. *American Journal of Psychiatry, 143,* 317–322.

Rickels, K., & Schweizer, E. E. (1986). Benzodiazepines for treatment of panic attacks: A new look. *Psychopharmacology Bulletin, 22,* 93–99.
IOCD—I

Robertson, J., Wendiggensen, P., & Kaplan, I. (1983). Toward a comprehensive treatment for obsessional thoughts. *Behaviour Research and Therapy, 21,* 347–356.

Rosenberg, C. (1967). Familial aspects of obsessional neurosis. *British Journal of Psychiatry, 113,* 405–413.

Rosenberg, H., & Upper, D. (1983). Problems with stimulus/response equivalence and reactivity in the assessment and treatment of obsessive–compulsive neurosis. *Behaviour Research and Therapy, 21,* 177–180.

Roth, M., & Mountjoy, C. Q. (1982). The distinction between anxiety states and depressive disorders. In E. S. Paykel (Ed.), *Handbook of affective disorders* (pp. 70–92). New York: Guilford.

Salkovskis, P. M. (1983). Treatment of an obsessional patient using habituation to audiotaped ruminations. *British Journal of Clinical Psychology, 22,* 311–313.

Salkovskis, P. M. (1985). Obsessional–compulsive problems: A cognitive-behavioural analysis. *Behaviour Research and Therapy, 23,* 571–583.

Salkovskis, P. M., & Warwick, H. M. C. (1985). Cognitive therapy of obsessive–compulsive disorder: Treating treatment failures. *Behavioural Psychotherapy, 13,* 243–255.

Sanavio, E., & Vidotto, G. (1985). The components of the Maudsley Obsessional–Compulsive Questionnaire. *Behaviour Research and Therapy, 23,* 659–662.

Sandler, J., & Hazari, A. (1960). The obsessional: Or the psychological classification of obsessional character traits and symptoms. *British Journal of Medical Psychology, 33,* 113–122.

Settle, E. C., Jr., & Settle, G. P. (1984). A case of mania associated with fluoxetine. *American Journal of Psychiatry, 141,* 280–281.

Shagass, C., Roemer, R. A., Straumanis, J. J., & Josiassen, R. C. (1984a). Distinctive somatosensory evoked potential features in obsessive–compulsive disorder. *Biological Psychiatry, 19,* 1507–1524.

Shagass, C., Roemer, R. A., Straumanis, J. J., & Josiassen, R. C. (1984b). Evoked potentials in obsessive–compulsive disorder. *Advances in Biological Psychiatry, 15,* 69–75.

Slade, P. D. (1974). Psychometric studies of obsessional illness and obsessional personality. In H. R. Beech (Ed.), *Obsessional states* (pp. 95–109). London: Methuen.

Snowdon, J. (1980). A comparison of written and postbox forms of the Leyton Obsessional Inventory. *Psychological Medicine, 10,* 165–170.

Solyom, L., Zamanyadek, D., Ledwick, B., & Kenny, F. (1971). Aversion relief treatment of obsessional neurosis. In R. Rubin (Ed.), *Advances in behavior therapy* (pp. 93–109). London: Academic Press.

Spring, B. J., & Zubin, J. (1978). Attention and information processing as indicators of vulnerability of schizophrenic episodes. *Journal of Psychiatric Research, 14,* 289–301.

Steketee, G. S., Foa, E. B., & Grayson, J. B. (1982). Recent advances in the treatment of obsessive–compulsives. *Archives of General Psychiatry, 39,* 1365–1371.

Stern, R. S. (1978). Obsessive thoughts: The problem of therapy. *British Journal of Psychiatry, 133,* 200–205.

Stern, R. S., & Cobb, J. P. (1978). Phenomenology of obsessive–compulsive neurosis. *British Journal of Psychiatry, 132,* 233–239.

Stern, R. S., Lipsedge, M. S., & Marks, I. M. (1975). Obsessive ruminations: A controlled trial of thought-stopping technique. *Behaviour Research and Therapy, 11,* 659–662.

Stern, T. A., & Jenike, M. A. (1983). Treatment of obsessive–compulsive disorder with lithium carbonate. *Psychosomatics, 24,* 671–673.

Sturgis, E. T., & Meyer, V. (1981). Obsessive–compulsive disorders. In S. M. Turner, K. S. Calhoun, & H. E. Adams (Eds.), *Handbook of clinical behavior therapy* (pp. 68–102). New York: John Wiley & Sons.

Tesar, G. E., & Jenike, M. A. (1984). Alprazolam as treatment for a case of obsessive–compulsive disorder. *American Journal of Psychiatry, 141,* 689–690.

Thoren, P., Asberg, M., Cronholm, B., Jornestedt, L., & Traskman, L. (1980). Clomipramine treatment of obsessive–compulsive disorder: I. A controlled clinical trial. *Archives of General Psychiatry, 37,* 1281–1285.

Thyer, B. A. (1985). Audio-taped exposure therapy in a case of obsessional neurosis. *Behaviour Therapy and Experimental Psychiatry, 16,* 271–273.

Turner, R. M., Newman, F. L., & Foa, E. B. (1983). Assessing the impact of cognitive differences in the treatment of obsessive–compulsives. *Journal of Clinical Psychology, 39,* 934–938.

Turner, S. M., Beidel, D. C., & Nathan, R. S. (1985). Biological factors in obsessive–compulsive disorder. *Psychological Bulletin, 97,* 430–450.

Turner, S. M., Beidel, D. C., Stanley, M. A., & Jacob, R. G. (in press). A comparison of fluoxetine and flooding in the treatment of obsessive–compulsive disorder. *Journal of Anxiety Disorders.*

Turner, S. M., Hersen, M., Bellack, A. S., & Wells, K. C. (1979). Behavioral treatment of obsessive–compulsive neurosis. *Behaviour Research and Therapy, 17,* 95–106.

Turner, S. M., Holzman, A., & Jacob, R. G. (1983). Treatment of compulsive looking by thought-stopping. *Behavior Modification, 7,* 576–582.

Turner, S. M., Jacob, R. G., Beidel, D. C., & Griffin, S. (1985). A second case of mania associated with fluoxetine. *American Journal of Psychiatry, 142,* 274–275.

Turner, S. M., Jacob, R. G., Beidel, D. C., & Himmelhoch, J. (1985). Fluoxetine treatment of obsessive–compulsive disorders. *Journal of Clinical Psychopharmacology, 5,* 207–212.

Turner, S. M., McCann, B. S., Beidel, D. C., & Mezzich, J. B. (1986). DSM-III classification of the anxiety disorders: A psychometric study. *Journal of Abnormal Psychology, 95,* 168–172.

Turner, S. M., & Michelson, L. (1984). Obsessive–compulsive disorders. In S. M. Turner (Ed.), *Behavioral theories and treatment of anxiety* (pp. 239–277). New York: Plenum.

Turns, D. M. (1985). Epidemiology of phobic and obsessive–compulsive disorders among adults. *American Journal of Psychotherapy, 39,* 360–370.

Vaughan, M. (1976). The relationships between obsessional personality, obsessions and depression and symptoms of depression. *British Journal of Psychiatry, 129,* 36–39.

Videbech, T. (1975). The psychopathology of anancastic endogenous depression. *Acta Psychiatria Scandinavia, 52,* 336–373.

Volavka, J., Neziroglu, F., & Yaryura-Tobias, J. A. (1985). Clomipramine and imipramine in obsessive–compulsive disorder. *Psychiatry Research, 14,* 83–91.

Walker, V. J., & Beech, H. R. (1969). Mood states and the ritualistic behavior of obsessional patients. *British Journal of Psychiatry, 115,* 1261–1268.

Walton, D., & Mather, M. D. (1963). The application of learning principles to the treatment of obsessive–compulsive states in the acute and chronic phases of illness. *Behaviour Research and Therapy, 1,* 163–174.

Warneke, L. B. (1984). The use of intravenous chlorimipramine in the treatment of obsessive–compulsive disorder. *Canadian Journal of Psychiatry, 29,* 135–141.

Welner, N., & Horowitz, M. (1975). Intrusive and repetitive thoughts after a depressing experience. *Psychological Reports, 37,* 135–138.

Yaryura-Tobias, J. A. (1977). Obsessive–compulsive disorders: A serotonergic hypothesis. *Journal of Orthomolecular Psychiatry, 6,* 317–326.

Yaryura-Tobias, J. A., & Bhagavan, H. N. (1977). L-Tryptophan in obsessive–compulsive disorders. *American Journal of Psychiatry, 134,* 1298–1299.

Zohar, J., & Insel, T. R. (1987). Obsessive–compulsive disorder: Psychobiological approaches to diagnosis, treatment, and pathophysiology. *Biological Psychiatry, 22,* 667–687.

Author Index

Author Index

Subject Index

About the Authors

Samuel M. Turner (Ph.D.) is Professor of Psychiatry, Director of the Anxiety Disorders Clinc and Director of the Western Psychiatric Institute and Clinic's Psychology Internship Program at the University of Pittsburgh School of Medicine. He is the Co-Editor for the *Journal of Psychopathology and Behavioral Assessment* and serves on the editorial board of several other scientific journals. The author of numerous journal publications, Dr. Turner is also the editor or co-editor of six books pertaining to psychopathology and behavioral treatment.

Deborah C. Beidel (Ph.D.) is a Post-Doctoral Fellow in Clinical Research at the University of Pittsburgh School of Medicine. She is the author or co-author of over twenty journal articles and several book chapters. She is a member of the editorial board of the *Journal of Psychopathology and Behavioral Assessment* and has served as a guest reviewer for numerous other scientific journals.

Psychology Practitioner Guidebooks

Editors
Arnold P. Goldstein, Syracuse University
Leonard Krasner, Stanford University & SUNY at Stony Brook
Sol L. Garfield, Washington University

Elsie M. Pinkston & Nathan L. Linsk — CARE OF THE ELDERLY: A Family Approach

Donald Meichenbaum — STRESS INOCULATION TRAINING

Sebastiano Santostefano — COGNITIVE CONTROL THERAPY WITH CHILDREN AND ADOLESCENTS

Lillie Weiss, Melanie Katzman & Sharlene Wolchik — TREATING BULIMIA: A Psychoeducational Approach

Edward B. Blanchard & Frank Andrasik — MANAGEMENT OF CHRONIC HEADACHES: A Psychological Approach

Raymond G. Romanczyk — CLINICAL UTILIZATION OF MICROCOMPUTER TECHNOLOGY

Philip H. Bornstein & Marcy T. Bornstein — MARITAL THERAPY: A Behavioral-Communications Approach

Michael T. Nietzel & Ronald C. Dillehay — PSYCHOLOGICAL CONSULTATION IN THE COURTROOM

Elizabeth B. Yost, Larry E. Beutler, M. Anne Corbishley & James R. Allender — GROUP COGNITIVE THERAPY: A Treatment Method for Depressed Older Adults

Lillie Weiss — DREAM ANALYSIS IN PSYCHOTHERAPY

Edward A. Kirby & Liam K. Grimley — UNDERSTANDING AND TREATING ATTENTION DEFICIT DISORDER

Jon Eisenson — LANGUAGE AND SPEECH DISORDERS IN CHILDREN

Eva L. Feindler & Randolph B. Ecton — ADOLESCENT ANGER CONTROL: Cognitive-Behavioral Techniques

Michael C. Roberts — PEDIATRIC PSYCHOLOGY: Psychological Interventions and Strategies for Pediatric Problems

Daniel S. Kirschenbaum, William G. Johnson & Peter M. Stalonas, Jr. —
TREATING CHILDHOOD AND ADOLESCENT OBESITY

W. Stewart Agras — EATING DISORDERS: Management of Obesity,
Bulimia and Anorexia Nervosa

Ian H. Gotlib & Catherine A. Colby — TREATMENT OF DEPRESSION:
An Interpersonal Systems Approach

Walter B. Pryzwansky & Robert N. Wendt — PSYCHOLOGY AS A
PROFESSION: Foundations of Practice

Cynthia D. Belar, William W. Deardorff & Karen E. Kelly — THE
PRACTICE OF CLINICAL HEALTH PSYCHOLOGY

Paul Karoly & Mark P. Jensen — MULTIMETHOD ASSESSMENT OF
CHRONIC PAIN

William L. Golden, E. Thomas Dowd & Fred Friedberg —
HYPNOTHERAPY: A Modern Approach

Patricia Lacks — BEHAVIORAL TREATMENT FOR PERSISTENT
INSOMNIA

Arnold P. Goldstein & Harold Keller — AGGRESSIVE BEHAVIOR:
Assessment and Intervention

C. Eugene Walker, Barbara L. Bonner & Keith L. Kaufman — THE
PHYSICALLY AND SEXUALLY ABUSED CHILD: Evaluation and
Treatment

Robert E. Becker, Richard G. Heimberg & Alan S. Bellack — SOCIAL
SKILLS TRAINING TREATMENT FOR DEPRESSION

Richard F. Dangel & Richard A. Polster — TEACHING CHILD
MANAGEMENT SKILLS

Albert Ellis, John F. McInerney, Raymond DiGiuseppe & Raymond
Yeager — RATIONAL-EMOTIVE THERAPY WITH ALCOHOLICS
AND SUBSTANCE ABUSERS

Johnny L. Matson & Thomas H. Ollendick — ENHANCING
CHILDREN'S SOCIAL SKILLS: Assessment and Training

Edward B. Blanchard, John E. Martin & Patricia M. Dubbert —
NON-DRUG TREATMENTS FOR ESSENTIAL HYPERTENSION

Samuel M. Turner & Deborah C. Beidel — TREATING OBSESSIVE–
COMPULSIVE DISORDER